Reteaching and Practice
Workbook

Grade 2

Scott Foresman·Addison Wesley

enVisionMATH
Common Core

PEARSON

Glenview, Illinois • Boston, Massachusetts • Chandler, Arizona • Upper Saddle River, New Jersey

ISBN-13: 978-0-328-79075-3

ISBN-10: 0-328-79075-3

5 6 7 8 9 10 V0N4 17 16 15

Contents

Writing Addition Number Sentences

How many counters are there in all?
Add the parts.

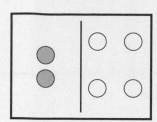

2 + 4 = 6
is called an
addition sentence.

_2_ and _4_ is _6_

Part   Part   Whole

_2_ plus _4_ equals _6_ .

_2_ + _4_ = _6_

Write the addition sentence for each problem.

1.

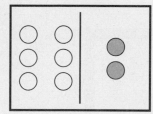

How many counters in all?

_6_ + _2_ = _8_

2.

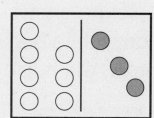

How many counters in all?

_7_ + _3_ = _10_

3.

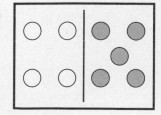

How many counters in all?

_4_ + _5_ = _9_

4.

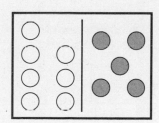

How many counters in all?

_7_ + _5_ = _12_

R 1·1

Name _____

Writing Addition Number Sentences

Write an addition sentence for the picture.

1.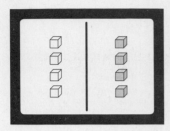

 $\underline{4} + \underline{4} = \underline{8}$

2.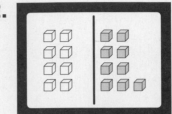

$\underline{8} + \underline{9} = \underline{12}$

3. Ann has 5 white rocks. She also has 6 gray rocks. Which picture shows how many white and gray rocks Ann has? 11

Ⓐ

Ⓑ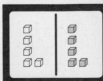

Ⓒ

Ⓓ

4. Algebra Write the missing number in the addition sentence.

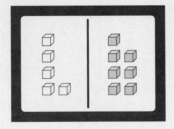

$\underline{5} + 7 = 12$

Stories About Joining

Follow the steps to solve this
joining story.

You have 6 red crayons.
Your teacher gives you 3 blue crayons.
How many crayons do you have in all?

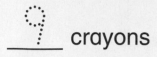 crayons

Write a number sentence for the story.

_6_ + _3_ = _9_

> 1. Draw 6 red crayons
>   in the box.
> 2. Draw 3 blue crayons
> 3. Count the crayons.

Draw a picture to solve each story problem.
Write a number sentence to go with each story.

1. There are 7 black cats
in the yard. 3 striped cats
join them. How many cats
are there in all?

2. You have 5 stickers.
Your friend gives you 6 more
stickers. How many stickers
do you have in all?

____ + ____ = ____   ____ + ____ = ____

Name _____

Stories About Joining

Draw a picture to find the sum.
Then write an addition sentence.

1. The monkey has 2 bananas.
He picks 9 more bananas.
How many bananas does
he have in all?

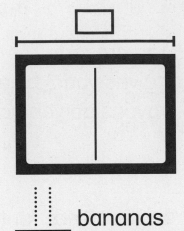

__2__ + __9__ = ____   __11__ bananas

2. Morgan has 3 pennies.
She finds some more
pennies. Now she has
11 pennies. How many
pennies did Morgan find?

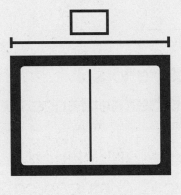

____ + ____ = ____   ____ pennies

3. Chad has 8 berries on his
pancake. 7 more berries
are in the bowl. How many
berries are there in all?

Ⓐ 8 berries

Ⓑ 10 berries

Ⓒ 15 berries

Ⓓ 18 berries

4. **Reasoning** Write a joining
story about the apples.
Use pictures, numbers,
or words.

P 1·2

Writing Subtraction Number Sentences

Count all the cubes. How many?

Now count the cubes with Xs.
How many cubes have Xs?

How many cubes are left?

Count the cubes.
Write a subtraction sentence.

1.

_____ − _____ = _____

2.

_____ − _____ = _____

3.

_____ − _____ = _____

4.

_____ − _____ = _____

5.

_____ − _____ = _____

6.

_____ − _____ = _____

7.

_____ − _____ = _____

8.

_____ − _____ = _____

R 1·3

Name _____

Writing Subtraction Number Sentences

Draw the missing part. Write a subtraction sentence.

1.

$$\boxed{7}$$

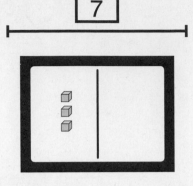

7 – 3 = ___

2.

$$\boxed{9}$$

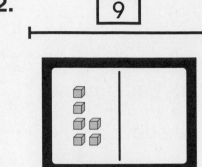

___ – ___ = ___

---

3. Kendra had 13 pencils. She took 4 pencils to school. Which subtraction sentence shows how many pencils Kendra left at home?

Ⓐ 17 – 4 = 13

Ⓑ 13 – 4 = 9

Ⓒ 13 – 9 = 4

Ⓓ 9 – 4 = 5

4. Spatial Thinking Draw a picture to show the story. Write a subtraction sentence.

14 mice are outside. Then 7 mice go back in the den. How many mice are still outside?

___ – ___ = ___

_____ mice

Stories About Separating

6 puppies are playing.
4 go home.
How many puppies are left?

$$6 - 4 = 2$$

Separate a group from the whole.
Then write a subtraction sentence.

1. There are 7 trucks in a lot.
5 trucks drive away.
How many trucks are left?

____ – ____ = ____

2. There are 8 apples.
You eat 3 apples.
How many apples are left?

____ – ____ = ____

3. Journal Write a separating story about cats.
Use pictures, numbers, or words. Show
the answer.

_____

_____

_____

Stories About Separating

Draw a picture to find the difference.
Write a subtraction sentence.

I. Pete has some stickers.
He uses 9 of them. Now he
has 7 stickers. How many
stickers did he have before?

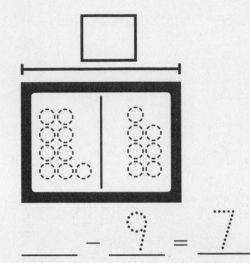

_16_ stickers

_____ − _9_ = _7_

---

2. Hong has 10 stamps. She
gives 6 stamps to Joe.
How many stamps does
she have left?

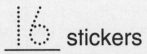

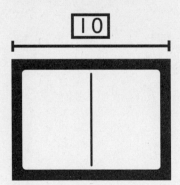

Ⓐ 4 stamps

Ⓑ 5 stamps

Ⓒ 6 stamps

Ⓓ 7 stamps

3. Reasonableness James
has 12 rocks. He puts
7 rocks in Maria's garden.
Which subtraction sentence
tells how many rocks he has
left?

Ⓐ 7 − 2 = 5

Ⓑ 7 − 4 = 3

Ⓒ 12 − 5 = 7

Ⓓ 12 − 7 = 5

Stories About Comparing

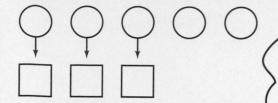

There are __5__ circles.

There are __3__ squares.

To compare the number of circles and squares, match each circle with a square. Are there more or fewer circles than squares?

How many *more* circles than squares? __2__

__5__ – __3__ = __2__

Draw a picture for each story.
Compare the pictures.
Write a subtraction sentence.

1. There are 6 flowers.
   There are 3 bees.
   How many *more* flowers
   than bees?

   ____ more flowers   ____ – ____ = ____

2. I have 7 juice boxes.
   I have 5 straws.
   How many *fewer* straws
   than juice boxes?

   ____ fewer straws   ____ – ____ = ____

Stories About Comparing

Draw a picture to find the difference.
Write a subtraction sentence.

1. A pond has 11 weeds and
7 lily pads. How many
more weeds than lily pads
does the pond have?

___4___ more weeds   __11__ – __7__ = __4__

2. A vine has 5 more red leaves
than brown leaves. The vine has
8 red leaves. How many brown
leaves does the vine have?

_____ brown leaves   _____ – _____ = _____

3. Mike plants 6 trees. Faye plants 4 trees.
How many fewer trees does Faye plant than Mike?

Ⓐ 2 fewer trees   Ⓒ 6 fewer trees

Ⓑ 4 fewer trees   Ⓓ 10 fewer trees

4. Journal Write a math story about
comparing to go with the picture.

_____

_____

_____

Connecting Addition and Subtraction

Finish the model.
Draw 6 dots to make one part.
Draw 3 dots to make the other part.

Show how the parts make the whole.
Write an addition sentence.

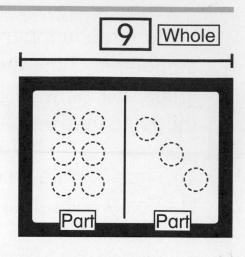

$$\underset{\text{Part}}{6} + \underset{\text{Part}}{3} = \underset{\text{Whole}}{9}$$

Write subtraction sentences.

$$9 - \underset{}{3} = 6$$
Whole   Part   Part

$$9 - \underset{}{6} = 3$$
Whole   Part   Part

Use the addition fact to help. The addition sentence tells the parts and the whole.

I. Add the parts to this model.
   Draw 7 dots and 5 dots.

2. Write number sentences for the model.

_____ + _____ = _____

_____ − _____ = _____

_____ − _____ = _____

Connecting Addition and Subtraction

1. Write three number
sentences about the
shirts. Fill in the
model to help you.

Tim has 5 white shirts.
He has 9 colored shirts.

14

5 + 9 = 14

___ − ___ = ___

___ − ___ = ___

---

2. Connie has 2 pairs of jeans.
She gets 3 more pairs of jeans.

Which number sentence
shows the story?

Ⓐ 2 + 3 = 5

Ⓑ 5 + 5 = 10

Ⓒ 3 − 2 = 1

Ⓓ 5 − 3 = 2

3. Number Sense Sarah had
5 caps. She lost 1 cap.

Which number sentence
shows the story?

Ⓐ 5 + 1 = 6

Ⓑ 1 + 6 = 7

Ⓒ 6 − 5 = 1

Ⓓ 5 − 1 = 4

Problem Solving: Use Objects

You can use counters and your workmat to solve this story problem.

5 frogs are on a rock.
3 frogs join them.
How many frogs in all?

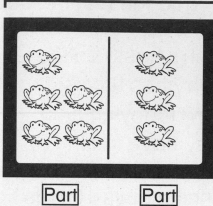

You need to find how many in all, or the whole.

Show 5 counters.
Show 3 more counters.
How many in all?

Do I need to add or subtract?
I will **add** because I need to find how many in all.

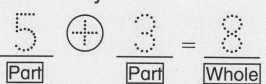

Use counters and your workmat to solve.
Circle add or subtract. Then write the number sentence.

I. 2 bugs are on a leaf.
4 bugs join them.
How many bugs in all?

add   or   subtract?

____ ◯ ____ = ____

2. 10 toads are in a pond.
5 toads jump out.
How many toads are left?

add   or   subtract?

____ ◯ ____ = ____

Name _____

Problem Solving: Use Objects

Use counters and a workmat.
Circle **add** or **subtract**.
Then write the number sentence.

1. Sierra has 3 cats.
Perry has 4 cats.
How many cats do
they have in all?

 subtract

   ____ cats

2. Annika buys 10 gifts.
Leroy buys 7 gifts.
Which number sentence
shows how many more gifts
Annika buys than Leroy?

Ⓐ $10 - 7 = 3$

Ⓑ $10 - 3 = 7$

Ⓒ $7 + 3 = 10$

Ⓓ $7 + 7 = 14$

3. 6 friends are playing a game.
Then some friends go home.
Now there are 2 friends
playing a game.
Which number sentence
matches this story?

Ⓐ $6 + 4 = 10$

Ⓑ $4 + 2 = 6$

Ⓒ $10 - 6 = 4$

Ⓓ $6 - 4 = 2$

4. Journal Write a math story. Then write a number
sentence to solve it.

_____

_____

◯   ◯

____   ____   ____

Adding 0, 1, 2

You can use a number line to add 0, 1, and 2.

Find 4 on the number line.
0 more than 4 is 4.

$4 + 0 =$ __4__

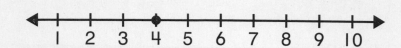

1 more than 4 is 5.

$4 + 1 =$ __5__

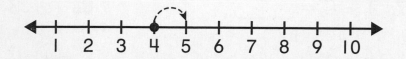

2 more than 4 is 6.

$4 + 2 =$ __6__

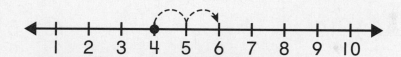

Add 0, 1, and 2.
Use the number line to help you.

1. $5 + 0 =$ ____

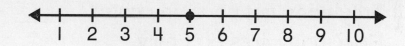

$5 + 1 =$ ____

$5 + 2 =$ ____

2. $7 + 0 =$ ____

$7 + 1 =$ ____

$7 + 2 =$ ____

R 2·1

Name _____

Adding 0, 1, 2

Circle the 0, 1, or 2. Then add.

1. 4
    +(2)
    ⋮
    6

2. 1
    + 6

3. 7
    + 2

4. 0
    + 8

5. 1 + 8 = ____

6. 0 + 5 = ____

7. 2 + 8 = ____

Ⓐ 8
Ⓑ 9
Ⓒ 10
Ⓓ 11

8. 1 + 3 = ____

Ⓐ 7
Ⓑ 6
Ⓒ 5
Ⓓ 4

9. Solve. Write a number sentence.

Emily has 4 cats.
Troy does not have any cats.
How many cats do Emily
and Troy have in all?

____ + ____ = ____

They have ____ cats in all.

Number Sense Add.

10. 4 + 0 = ____   0 + 6 = ____   5 + 0 = ____

11. What pattern do you notice in your answers?

_____

12. Use your pattern to find these sums.

17 + 0 = ____   0 + 89 = ____   253 + 0 = ____

Doubles

Find 3 + 3.

Draw 3 more dots to show the double.
Then write the addition sentence.

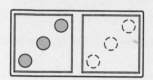

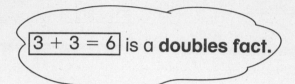

$3 + 3 = 6$ is a **doubles fact.**

_3_ + _3_ = _6_

Draw dots on the domino to show the double.
Then write the addition sentence.

1.

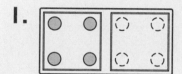

$4 +$ _4_ $=$ _8_

2.

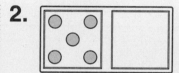

$5 +$ ___ $=$ ___

3.

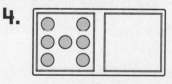

___ $+$ ___ $=$ ___

4.

___ $+$ ___ $=$ ___

5.

___ $+$ ___ $=$ ___

6.

___ $+$ ___ $=$ ___

Name _____

Doubles

Complete the doubles.
Then solve.

1.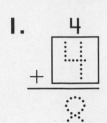
```
   4
+  4
─────
   8
```

2.
```
  [ ]
+  6
─────
```

3.
```
   2
+ [ ]
─────
```

4.
```
  [ ]
+  9
─────
```

5. 8 + [ ] = ____

6. [ ] + 5 = ____

7. 3 + 3 = ____

Ⓐ 8

Ⓑ 7

Ⓒ 6

Ⓓ 5

8. 7 + 7 = ____

Ⓐ 10

Ⓑ 11

Ⓒ 12

Ⓓ 14

9. Juana has two boxes of chalk. Each box has 8 pieces of chalk.

Which addition fact shows the problem?

Ⓐ 4 + 4 = 8

Ⓑ 8 + 0 = 8

Ⓒ 7 + 9 = 16

Ⓓ 8 + 8 = 16

10. Reasoning Jim has 6 toy cars. Carl has the same number of cars.

How many cars does Carl have?

Ⓐ 6

Ⓑ 10

Ⓒ 12

Ⓓ 16

Near Doubles

You can use a doubles fact to solve a near doubles fact.

To solve a near doubles fact, add I more to the doubles fact.

6 + 6 = 12   6 + 7 = 13
Doubles Fact   **Near Doubles Fact**

---

1. Write and solve the doubles facts and the near doubles facts.

   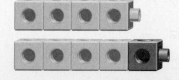

____ + ____ = ____   ____ + ____ = ____

2.

____ + ____ = ____   ____ + ____ = ____

3. Journal Draw pictures of cubes to show the facts. Then solve.

7 + 7 = ____   7 + 8 = ____
Doubles Fact   **Near Doubles Fact**

Near Doubles

Add. Use the doubles facts to help you.

1.
$$\begin{array}{r} 4 \\ + 4 \\ \hline 8 \end{array} \qquad \begin{array}{r} 4 \\ + 5 \\ \hline \end{array}$$

2.
$$\begin{array}{r} 6 \\ + 6 \\ \hline \end{array} \qquad \begin{array}{r} 6 \\ + 7 \\ \hline \end{array}$$

3. $8 + 8 = $ _____ $8 + 9 = $ _____

4. Solve.

Terry's doll house has 7 windows on the first floor and 8 windows on the second floor.

Which number sentence shows how many windows in all?

Ⓐ $7 + 1 = 8$

Ⓑ $7 + 7 = 14$

Ⓒ $7 + 8 = 15$

Ⓓ $8 + 8 = 16$

5. **Spatial Thinking** Draw a picture to show the story. Then write an addition sentence for the story.

Jane has 5 books.
Fred has 6 books.

How many books in all?

_____ + _____ = _____

_____ books

Adding in Any Order

You can add two numbers in any order.
The answer is the same.

5 + 2 = __7__   2 + 5 = __7__

5 + 2 = 7 and 2 + 5 = 7 are turn-around facts.

Write number sentences for each picture.
Solve the turn-around facts.

1.

   ___ + ___ = ___   ___ + ___ = ___

2.

   ___ + ___ = ___   ___ + ___ = ___

3.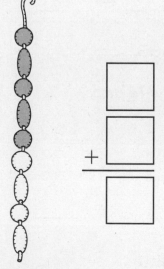

   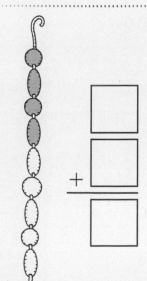

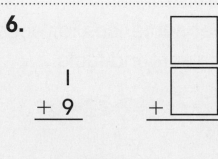
Adding in Any Order

Write the sum. Then write the turn-around fact.

1. 4 + 6 = 10

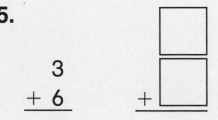

6 + 4 = 10

2. 5 + 3 = ____

____ + ____ = ____

3. 9 + 4 = ____

____ + ____ = ____

4. 2 + 5 = ____

____ + ____ = ____

5.

3
+ 6

+ ☐

6.

1
+ 9

+ ☐

Solve. Write two turn-around facts.

7. A farm has 7 horses.
It gets 2 more horses.
How many horses does
the farm have now?

____ + ____ = ____

____ + ____ = ____

____ horses

8. Geometry Which shape belongs in the sentence?

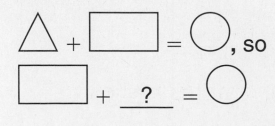

 Ⓐ ◯

 Ⓑ △

Ⓒ ▭

 Ⓓ ⬡

Adding Three Numbers

There are different ways to add three numbers.

You can add any two numbers or try to make 10.
You can also look for doubles or near doubles.
Then add the third number.

Add any 2 numbers.   **Try to make 10.**   **Look for doubles.**

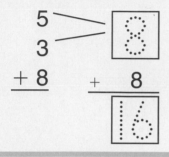

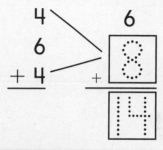

Find the sums.
Draw lines from the first two numbers you add.

1.   7   4   **2.**   8   ☐   **3.**   1   6
         4   2   6
       + 3   + [☐]   + 5   +   5   + 9   +

4.   7   ☐   **5.**   8   4   **6.**   2   2
         7   4   6
       + 5   +   5   + 8   +   + 7   +

7. Journal Use pictures, numbers, or words to show
   two different ways to add 2 + 4 + 6.

Name ______________________

Practice
2-5

Adding Three Numbers

Write the sum.
Circle the numbers you added first.

1.
$$\begin{array}{r} 4 \\ 3 \\ +\ 2 \\ \hline 9 \end{array}$$

2.
$$\begin{array}{r} 6 \\ 0 \\ +\ 5 \\ \hline \end{array}$$

3.
$$\begin{array}{r} 2 \\ 9 \\ +\ 2 \\ \hline \end{array}$$

4.
$$\begin{array}{r} 7 \\ 4 \\ +\ 1 \\ \hline \end{array}$$

5. 7 + 6 + 3 = ____

6. 5 + 0 + 6 = ____

7. 3 + 7 + 5 = ____

Ⓐ 10
Ⓑ 14
Ⓒ 15
Ⓓ 16

8. 3 + 8 + 2 = ____

Ⓐ 13
Ⓑ 12
Ⓒ 11
Ⓓ 10

9. Lila cut out 3 rainbows.
She cut out 4 moons.
She cut out 7 stars.
How many shapes did Lila cut out in all?

Ⓐ 7
Ⓑ 10
Ⓒ 11
Ⓓ 14

10. Algebra Add across and down. Write the missing numbers.

9	3	2	14
	6		14
1		8	14
14	14	14	

Name _____

Making 10 to Add

This shows 8 + 4.

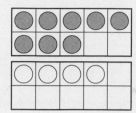

Show 10 + 2.
Move 2 counters to make 10.

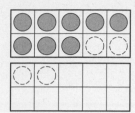

8 + 4 is the same as 10 + 2.

8 + 4 = 12

10 + 2 = 12

Make 10 to help you add.

1. Find 9 + 7.

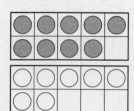

Move 1 counter to make 10.

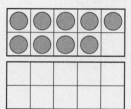

9 + 7 is the same as 10 + 6.

9 + 7 = 16

___ + ___ = ___

2. Find 7 + 5.

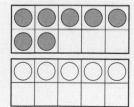

Move 3 counters to make 10.

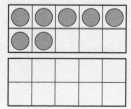

7 + 5 is the same as 10 + 2.

___ + ___ = ___

___ + ___ = ___

Name _____

Making 10 to Add

Make 10 to add.
Use counters and your workmat.

1.   8
   + 3

2.   5
   + 6

3.   7
   + 9

4.   6
   + 7

5.   9
   + 1

6.   4
   + 8

7.   2
   + 9

8.   0
   + 8

---

9. 5 + 8 = _____

10. 7 + 7 = _____

11. Jay has 6 yellow blocks.
He has 8 green blocks.
How many blocks does
Jay have in all?

Ⓐ 13

Ⓑ 14

Ⓒ 15

Ⓓ 16

12. Tia has 9 blue pens.
She has 4 red pens.
How many pens does
Tia have in all?

Ⓐ 15

Ⓑ 14

Ⓒ 13

Ⓓ 12

13. Writing in Math Use counters. Tell how to make 10 when
adding 8 + 5.

_____

_____

_____

Name _____

Problem Solving: Draw a Picture and Write a Number Sentence

Tim and Rose played two games. How many points in all did Tim and Rosa score in Game 1?

Players	Game 1	Game 2
Tim	////	//
Rosa	卌	卌 /

Use a part-part-whole mat to find out.

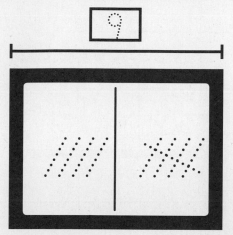

Write a number sentence.

$$\underset{\text{Tim}}{4} + \underset{\text{Rosa}}{5} = \underset{\text{Points in all}}{9}$$

In game 1, Tim and Rosa scored __9__ points in all.

Use a part-part-whole mat and write a number sentence to solve.

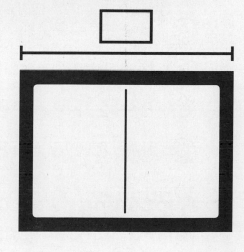

1. How many points in all did Tim and Rosa score in Game 2?

2.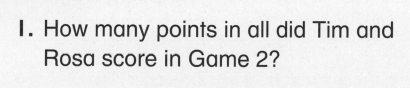
$$\underset{\text{Tim}}{\underline{\quad}} + \underset{\text{Rosa}}{\underline{\quad}} = \underset{\text{Points in all}}{\underline{\quad}}$$

3. In game 2, Tim and Rosa scored _____ points in all.

Name _____

Problem Solving: Draw a Picture and Write a Number Sentence

Three children made a table to show how many stickers they have.

Stickers Collected			
	☺	🌈	🐕
Fernando	8	0	9
Kathleen	4	8	6
Mohammed	5	7	3

1. Draw counters and write a number sentence to solve. How many stickers does Fernando have?

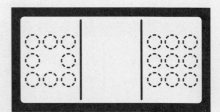

_8_ + _0_ + _9_ = _17_ stickers

2. Which number sentence tells how many stickers Kathleen has?

Ⓐ 8 − 4 = 4

Ⓑ 4 + 8 + 2 = 14

Ⓒ 8 + 2 + 6 = 16

Ⓓ 4 + 8 + 6 = 18

3. Which number sentence tells how many stickers Mohammed has?

Ⓐ 5 + 7 = 12

Ⓑ 7 + 7 + 7 = 21

Ⓒ 5 + 7 + 3 = 15

Ⓓ 5 + 7 + 6 = 18

4. Reasoning Draw counters and write a number sentence to show how many 🐕 the children have in all.

___ + ___ + ___ = ___

P 2•7

Subtracting 0, 1, 2

You can use a number line to subtract 0, 1, and 2.

Find 6 on the number line.
0 less than 6 is 6.

6 − 0 = _6_

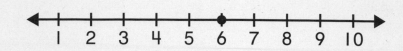

1 less than 6 is 5.

6 − 1 = _5_

2 less than 6 is 4.

6 − 2 = _4_

Subtract 0, 1, and 2.
Use the number line to help you.

1. 4 − 0 = ____

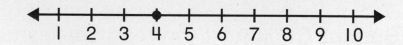

    4 − 1 = ____

    4 − 2 = ____

2. 7 − 0 − ____

    7 − 1 = ____

    7 − 2 = ____

Name _____

Subtracting 0, 1, 2

Solve. Use cubes if needed.

1.   7
    − 2
    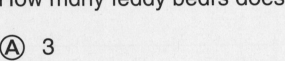

2.   5
    − 1

3.   2
    − 0

4.   1
    − 1

5. 4 − 0 = _____

6. 10 − 2 = _____

---

7. Kim has 5 teddy bears.
Jill has 1 less teddy bear than Kim.
How many teddy bears does Jill have?

Ⓐ 3

Ⓑ 4

Ⓒ 5

Ⓓ 6

---

8. Spatial Thinking Draw a picture to show the story.
Write a subtraction sentence.

Ted takes a card with
the number 10 on it.
Li takes a card with a
number that is 2 less than 10.

What number did Li take?

Li takes the number _____.   _____ − _____ = _____

Name _____

Thinking Addition to Subtract Doubles

6 − 3 = ?

Think of a doubles fact.

3 + _3_ = 6    So, 6 − 3 = _3_.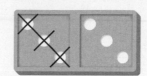

Use doubles facts to help you subtract.
Cross out the dots you take away.

1. 8 − 4 = ?

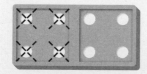

4 + _4_ = 8   8 − 4 = _4_

2. 10 − 5 = ?

5 + ____ = 10   10 − 5 = ____

3. 12 − 6 = ?

6 + ____ = 12 12 − 6 = ____

4. 14 − 7 = ?

7 + ____ = 14 14 − 7 = ____

5. 16 − 8 = ?

8 + ____ = 16 16 − 8 = ____

6. 18 − 9 = ?

9 + ____ = 18 18 − 9 = ____

Thinking Addition to Subtract Doubles

Subtract. Write the doubles fact that helped you.
Use cubes if you need to.

1.

$$\begin{array}{r} 4 \\ -2 \\ \hline 2 \end{array}$$

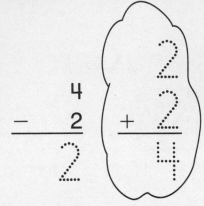

$$\begin{array}{r} 2 \\ +2 \\ \hline 4 \end{array}$$

2.

$$\begin{array}{r} 12 \\ -6 \\ \hline \end{array}$$

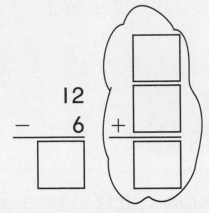

3. $16 - 8 =$ _____

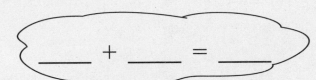

_____ $+$ _____ $=$ _____

4. $18 - 9 =$ _____

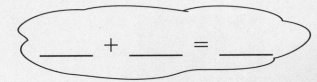

_____ $+$ _____ $=$ _____

5. David had 6 pizzas at his party.
His friends ate 3 pizzas.
Which doubles fact could you use
to find how many pizzas are left?

Ⓐ $3 + 3 = 6$

Ⓑ $6 + 6 = 12$

Ⓒ $6 - 6 = 0$

Ⓓ $6 + 3 = 9$

6. Reasoning Krista and Alan have 8 bookmarks.
How could they share the bookmarks so that they
each have the same number?

_____

Name _____

Thinking Addition to 10 to Subtract

Addition facts can help you subtract.
Use the pictures to find the missing numbers.

Addition Fact	**Subtraction Fact**

Think $2 +$ __8__ $= 10$.	So, $10 - 2 =$ __8__

Use addition facts to help you subtract.

1.

Think $3 +$ ____ $= 7$.   So, $7 - 3 =$ ____.

2.

Think $7 +$ ____ $= 8$.   So, $8 - 7 =$ ____.

3.

Think $6 +$ ____ $= 10$.   So, $10 - 6 =$ ____.

Name _____

Thinking Addition to 10 to Subtract

Use addition facts to help you subtract.
Use counters if you need to.

1.

$$\begin{array}{r} 8 \\ -\ 3 \\ \hline 5 \end{array}$$

$$\begin{array}{r} 3 \\ +\ 5 \\ \hline 8 \end{array}$$

2.

$$\begin{array}{r} 10 \\ -\ 6 \\ \hline \square \end{array}$$

$$\begin{array}{r} 6 \\ +\ \square \\ \hline 10 \end{array}$$

3. $9 - 6 =$ _____

$6 +$ _____ $= 9$

4. $6 - 2 =$ _____

$2 +$ _____ $= 6$

....

5. Number Sense Chris has 7 whistles.
He needs 10 whistles for his party.
Which number sentence can help you find how
many more whistles Chris needs?

Ⓐ $7 + 10 = 17$

Ⓑ $7 - 3 = 4$

Ⓒ $7 + 3 = 10$

Ⓓ $4 + 3 = 7$

Thinking Addition to 18 to Subtract

Addition facts can help you subtract.
Use the pictures to find the missing numbers.

Addition Fact

Think 6 +  = 14.

Subtraction Fact

So, 14 − 6 = _8_

Think addition to help you subtract.

1.

Think 9 + ____ = 13.

So, 13 − 9 = ____.

2.

Think 7 + ____ = 15.

So, 15 − 7 = ____.

3.

Think 8 + ____ = 17.

So, 17 − 8 = ____.

4. Algebra Use a related addition fact to complete
the subtraction fact.

11 − ____ = 2

2 + ____ = 11

Thinking Addition to 18 to Subtract

Use addition facts to help you subtract.
Use counters if you need to.

1.

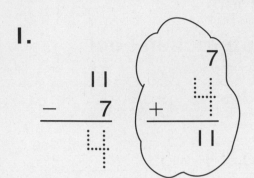

$$\begin{array}{r} 11 \\ -\ \ 7 \\ \hline 4 \end{array} \qquad \begin{array}{r} 7 \\ +\ 4 \\ \hline 11 \end{array}$$

2. $15 - 6 = $ _____

$6 +$ _____ $= 15$

3. Maria had 11 rings. She lost 3 rings.
   Which addition fact can help you find how many
   rings Maria has left?

   Ⓐ $3 + 1 = 4$

   Ⓑ $6 + 5 = 11$

   Ⓒ $3 + 8 = 11$

   Ⓓ $11 + 3 = 14$

4. **Journal** Write a subtraction story for $12 - 9$.
   Then write the addition fact that can help you solve
   your story.

   _____

   _____

   _____

   ___ $+$ ___ $=$ ___ $12 - 9 = $ ___

Making 10 to Subtract

Making 10 can help you subtract.

To find 13 − 5, show 13.

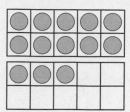

Subtract 3 to make a 10.

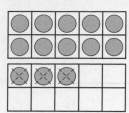

You need to subtract a total of 5 counters,
so subtract 2 more counters.

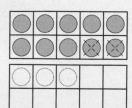

There are 8 counters left.

So, 13 − 5 = _8_.

Use counters and your workmat to subtract.

1. 11 − 7 = _4_

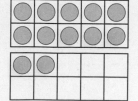

2. 14 − 6 = ____

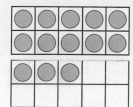

3. 12 − 5 = ____

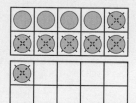

4. 13 − 7 = ____

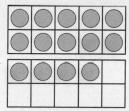

Making 10 to Subtract

Make a 10 to subtract.
Use counters and your workmat.

1.   11
      $-\ 5$

2.   15
      $-\ 6$

3.   11
      $-\ 9$

4.   12
      $-\ 6$

5.   16
      $-\ 8$

6.   12
      $-\ 9$

7.   13
      $-\ 4$

8.   17
      $-\ 9$

9.   14
      $-\ 9$

10.   13
       $-\ 8$

11.   11
       $-\ 4$

12.   18
       $-\ 9$

13. Number Sense Which subtraction
sentences show you how to find $15 - 7$?

(A) $15 - 6 = 9,$ $9 - 8 = 1$

(B) $15 - 5 = 10,$ $10 - 5 = 5$

(C) $15 - 5 = 10,$ $10 - 2 = 8$

(D) $15 - 2 = 13,$ $13 - 2 = 11$

Name _____

Problem Solving:
Two-Question Problems

Write the number sentences to solve both parts.

Jenna has 3 red markers and 5 blue markers.
How many markers does she have in all?

Part 1

Add to find out how many markers Jenna has in all.

$$\underline{3} \ \oplus \ \underline{5} = \underline{8}$$

Then Jenna lost 2 markers. How many markers does Jenna have left?

Part 2

Subtract the number of markers Jenna lost.

$$\underline{8} \ \ominus \ \underline{2} = \underline{6}$$

Jenna has __6__ markers left.

Remember: You have to solve the first part before you can solve the second part.

Write the number sentences to solve both parts.

1. There are 5 red apples and 4 green apples in a bowl. How many apples are in the bowl?

Part 1

$$\underline{5} \ \oplus \ \underline{4} = \underline{}$$

____ apples

Eric ate 1 of the apples. How many apples are in the bowl now?

Part 2

$$\underline{} \ \ominus \ \underline{} = \underline{}$$

____ apples

Name _____

Problem Solving:
Two-Question Problems

Write the number sentences to solve both parts.

1. Kendra drew 5 pictures. She threw 2 pictures away. How many pictures did she keep?

____ ◯ ____ = ____

Then Kendra drew 7 more pictures. How many pictures does she have now?

____ ◯ ____ = ____

2. Troy had 6 apples. He gave 4 apples away. How many apples does he have left?

____ ◯ ____ = ____

Troy picked 3 more apples. How many apples does he have now?

____ ◯ ____ = ____

Mark the number sentences that match the story.

3. Jo buys 2 green cars and 7 red cars. How many cars does she buy? Then Jo buys 5 yellow cars. How many cars does she have now?

Ⓐ 5 + 2 = 7
    7 + 5 = 12

Ⓑ 2 + 7 = 9
    9 + 5 = 14

Ⓒ 7 + 2 = 9
    9 − 5 = 4

Ⓓ 7 − 2 = 5
    5 − 5 = 0

4. Reuben checked 9 books out of the library. He returned 3 of the books. How many books does he have left?

____ ◯ ____ = ____

Then Reuben returned 3 more books. How many books does he have now?

____ ◯ ____ = ____

Name _____

Repeated Addition

Add equal groups to find how many in all.

_2_ + _2_ + _2_ + _2_ = a **sum** of _8_

---

1. Number Sense Draw dots to show equal groups.
Find the sum.

3 + 3 + 3 = ____   [ ] [ ] [ ]

....

Find the sum.

2.

4 + 4 + 4 + 4 = ____

....

3.

5 + 5 + 5 + 5 + 5 = ____

....

4.

4 + 4 + 4 + 4 + 4 = ____

R 4·1

Repeated Addition

Use the model.
Complete each sentence.

1. ? in all

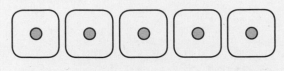

1 + 1 + 1 + 1 + 1 = 5

2. ? in all

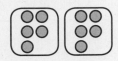

5 + 5 = ____

3. ? in all

3 + 3 + 3 = ____

4. ? in all

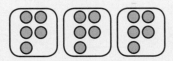

5 + 5 + 5 = ____

5. 2 monkeys climb a tree.
Each monkey picks 3 bananas.

Which number sentence shows this problem?

2 + 3	2 + 2	3 + 3	3 + 3 + 3
Ⓐ	Ⓑ	Ⓒ	Ⓓ

6. Number Sense Find the sum.
Write an addition sentence
to show the same amount.

5 + 5 + 5 + 5 = ____

Building Arrays

A collection of objects arranged in equal rows and columns is an **array.** You can use an **array** to show equal groups.

Array

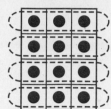

Circle each row. Count the number of rows.

There are __4__ rows.
Count the number of dots in each row.

There are __3__ dots in each row.
Write the addition sentence.

__3__ + __3__ + __3__ + __3__ = __12__

Circle each row. Count the number of rows.
Count the number of dots in each row.
Write the addition sentence.

I.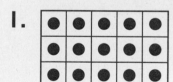

There are _____ rows.

There are _____ dots in each row.

_____ + _____ + _____ = _____

2.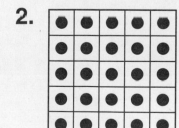

There are _____ rows.

There are _____ dots in each row.

___ + ___ + ___ + ___ + ___ = ___

Name _____

Building Arrays

Write the addition sentence.

1.

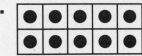 =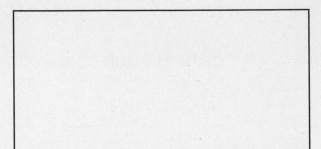

_3_ + _3_ = _6_

2.

__ + __ + __ = __

3.

____ + ____ = ____

4.

__ + __ + __ = __

5. Mrs. Rose takes cookies out of the oven.
They are in 4 rows and 5 columns.

Which addition sentence
shows how many cookies in all?

$4 + 5 = 9$ $4 + 4 + 4 = 12$ $5 + 5 + 5 + 5 = 20$ $5 + 5 + 5 + 5 + 5 = 25$
   (A)   (B)   (C)   (D)

6. Spatial Thinking Draw an array with 2 rows and
4 columns. Then write a number sentence for your array.

____ + ____ = ____

Practicing Repeated Addition

2 + 2 + 2 + 2 + 2 = ?

I put my cars in rows. Next, I see how many cars are in each row. Then, I use repeated addition to find out how many cars I have.

__2__ + __2__ + __2__ + __2__ + __2__ = __10__

Write an addition sentence to match the array.

1. __5__ + __5__ + __5__ + __5__ = __20__

2. ____ + ____ + ____ = ____

Practicing Repeated Addition

Write a repeated addition sentence to solve each problem.

1. Carolina has 3 shelves in her room. She puts 4 stuffed animals on each shelf. How many stuffed animals does Carolina have in her room?

_____ + _____ + _____ = _____

2. Juan puts pictures in 2 rows in his photo album. He puts 2 pictures in each row. How many pictures does Juan have?

_____ + _____ = _____

3. Mrs. Kim places chairs in her classroom in 4 rows. She puts 3 chairs in each row. How many chairs are in Mrs. Kim's classroom?

_____ + _____ + _____ + _____ = _____

4. **Number Sense** Which number sentence shows 3 rows with 5 in each row?

Ⓐ 5 + 5 + 5 + 5 = 20

Ⓑ 5 + 5 + 5 = 15

Ⓒ 3 + 3 + 3 = 9

Ⓓ 3 + 5 = 8

Problem Solving: Draw a Picture and Write a Number Sentence

You can draw a picture to solve a problem.
First, read the problem.

Fran knits 4 mittens.
Each mitten has 5 buttons.
How many buttons are there in all?

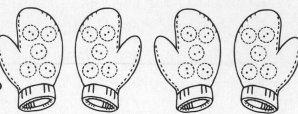

Next, draw 5 buttons on each mitten.

Then, write a number sentence.

$$5 + 5 + 5 + 5 = 20$$

Draw a picture to solve.
Then write a number sentence.

1. There are 6 vases.
   Each vase has 3 flowers.
   How many flowers are there in all?

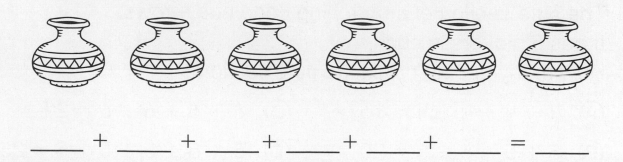

___ + ___ + ___ + ___ + ___ + ___ = ___

Name _____

Problem Solving: Draw a Picture and Write a Number Sentence

Write number sentences to solve the problems.
Make part-part-whole drawings to help.

1. Zach buys 3 packs of tapes. Each pack has 3 tapes. How many tapes does he buy in all?

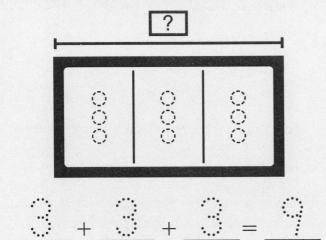

_3_ + _3_ + _3_ = _9_

2. Carlos makes 2 books. Each book has 6 pages. How many pages did Carlos make in all?

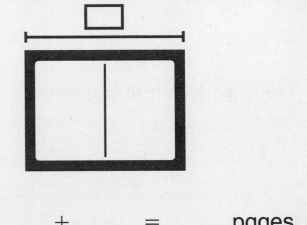

____ + ____ = ____ pages

3. Nell has 2 baskets. She has 9 toys in each basket. How many toys does she have in all?

16 toys	17 toys	18 toys	19 toys
Ⓐ	Ⓑ	Ⓒ	Ⓓ

4. Reasoning Which number sentence will solve the problem?

The flute section of a marching band has 4 rows.
It has 5 players in each row.
How many people are in the flute section?

Ⓐ $4 + 4 + 4 + 4 = 16$ Ⓒ $6 + 6 + 6 + 6 = 24$

Ⓑ $5 + 5 + 5 + 5 = 20$ Ⓓ $5 + 5 + 5 + 5 + 5 = 25$

Name _____

Models for Tens and Ones

Ally had 35 raisins to make a snack.
She grouped the raisins into tens and ones.

The raisins on the celery show tens.

The leftover raisins show the ones.

I ten   I ten   I ten   ones

__3__ tens and __5__ ones is __35__.

Count the tens and ones.
Write the numbers.

1.

_____ ten and _____ ones is _____.

2.

_____ tens and _____ ones is _____.

3.

_____ tens and _____ ones is _____.

Models for Tens and Ones

Circle groups of ten.
Tell how many tens and ones.
Write the number.

1.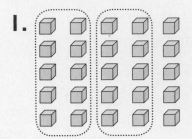

_2_ tens _5_ ones

_25_

2.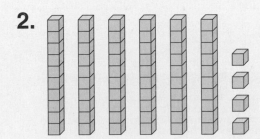

____ tens ____ ones

____

3. Sharon cut open this watermelon. How many seeds can you see?

____ tens ____ ones

____

4. Estimation Terry has about 20 keys.

Which number could be the exact number of keys that Terry has?

(A) 9

(B) 21

(C) 35

(D) 42

Reading and Writing Numbers

Ones	Teens	Tens
1 one	11 eleven	10 ten
2 two	12 twelve	20 twenty
3 three	13 thirteen	30 thirty
4 four	14 fourteen	40 forty
5 five	15 fifteen	50 fifty
6 six	16 sixteen	60 sixty
7 seven	17 seventeen	70 seventy
8 eight	18 eighteen	80 eighty
9 nine	19 nineteen	90 ninety

Write the number.

7 tens and 8 ones is _78_.

78 has two **digits**.

Write the number word.

seventy and **eight** is

seventy-eight

Write the number and the number word.

1. 2 tens and 9 ones is ____. _____

2. 6 tens and 3 ones is ____. _____

3. 9 tens and 2 ones is ____. _____

4. 8 tens and 6 ones is ____. _____

Number Sense What is the number?

5. It is greater than 43 and less than 52. If you add the digits, the sum is 8. Write the number word.

_____

6. It is less than 60 and greater than 55. If you add the digits, the sum is 13. Write the number.

____

Name _____

Reading and Writing Numbers

Write the number.

1. forty-two 42

2. sixty-five ____

3. fifteen ____

4. fifty-one ____

Write the number word.

5. 33 thirty-three

6. 17 _____

7. 57 _____

8. 26 _____

9. 48 _____

10. 39 _____

11. What number do the cubes show?

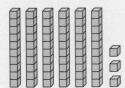

Ⓐ ten

Ⓑ thirty-six

Ⓒ sixty

Ⓓ sixty-three

12. **Number Sense** Write the number word to solve the riddle.

I am greater than 4 tens and less than 5 tens. I have 9 ones. What number am I?

_____

Using Symbols
to Compare Numbers

Compare numbers using >, <, and =.

> means "is greater than".
< means "is less than".
= means "equal to".

Tens	Ones
3	4

34 > 32

is greater than

Tens	Ones
3	2

Tens	Ones
3	2

32 < 34

is less than

Tens	Ones
3	4

Tens	Ones
3	2

32 = 32

is equal to

Tens	Ones
3	2

Write less than, greater than, or equal to.
Circle >, <, or =.

1. 13 is _____ 31.

13   >   <   =   31

2. 24 is _____ 24.

24   >   <   =   24

3. 67 is _____ 57.

67   >   <   =   57

4. 63 is _____ 74.

63   >   <   =   74

Using Symbols to Compare Numbers

Write >, <, or = in the ◯.

1. 17 ◁ 21

2. 59 ◯ 54

3. 29 ◯ 29

4. 12 ◯ 21

5. Solve. Write the numbers. Write <, > or = in the ◯. A toy store has 38 red spiders. It has 43 black spiders. Does it have more red spiders or black spiders?

_____ ◯ _____

more _____ spiders

6. A blue jar has 25 marbles. A red jar has 53 marbles. Which shows how to compare the number of marbles?

Ⓐ 25 = 53

Ⓑ 25 > 53

Ⓒ 53 < 25

Ⓓ 53 > 25

7. Journal One box holds 16 crayons. Another box holds 24 crayons. Write a sentence using words that compares the crayons in the two boxes.

_____

_____

_____

Then write a number sentence that compares the two boxes. Use > or <.

_____ ◯ _____

Counting to 100

1	2	3	4	5	6	7	8	9	10
11	12	13	14	15	16	17	18	19	20
21	22	23	24	25	26	27	28	29	30
31	32	33	34	35	36	37	38	39	40
41	42	43	44	45	46	47	48	49	50
51	52	53	54	55	56	57	58	59	60
61	62	63	64	65	66	67	68	69	70
71	72	73	74	75	76	77	78	79	80
81	82	83	84	85	86	87	88	89	90
91	92	93	94	95	96	97	98	99	100

Use the words **before** and **after** to help you find the numbers.

One **before** 66 is 65.

One **after** 66 is 67.

Count on from 66.

66, 67, 68, 69

Count back from 66.

66, 65, 64, 63

Write the numbers.

1. One before 12 is _____.

2. One after 70 is _____.

3. One after 45 is _____.

4. One before 91 is _____.

5. Count on from 23. Write the missing numbers.

23, _____, _____, _____

6. Count back from 87. Write the missing numbers.

87, _____, _____, _____

Counting to 100

Write the number that is 1 before or 1 after.
You can use the hundred chart to help.

Before   1. 62 , 63   2. _____, 51

After   3. 39, _____   4. 98, _____

Count on and count back to write the missing numbers.

5. _____, _____, _____, 64   6. 78, _____, _____, _____

7. The number on the white cap is
    1 more than 52 and 1 less than 54.
    What number goes on the white cap?

1	2	3	4	5	6	7	8	9	10
11	12	13	14	15	16	17	18	19	20
21	22	23	24	25	26	27	28	29	30
31	32	33	34	35	36	37	38	39	40
41	42	43	44	45	46	47	48	49	50
51	52	53	54	55	56	57	58	59	60
61	62	63	64	65	66	67	68	69	70
71	72	73	74	75	76	77	78	79	80
81	82	83	84	85	86	87	88	89	90
91	92	93	94	95	96	97	98	99	100

   Ⓐ 25

   Ⓑ 35

   Ⓒ 53

   Ⓓ 55

8. What number is it?
    The number is **after** 45
    and **before** 47.

   Ⓐ 74

   Ⓑ 48

   Ⓒ 46

   Ⓓ 44

9. **Spatial Thinking** Which
    number comes **10 after**
    76 on the hundred chart?

   Ⓐ 77

   Ⓑ 85

   Ⓒ 86

   Ⓓ 87

10 More or 10 Less

1	2	3	4	5	6	7	8	9	10
11	12	13	14	15	16	17	18	19	20
21	22	23	24	25	26	27	28	29	30
31	32	33	34	35	36	37	38	39	40
41	42	43	44	45	46	47	48	49	50
51	52	53	54	55	56	57	58	59	60
61	62	63	64	65	66	67	68	69	70
71	72	73	74	75	76	77	78	79	80
81	82	83	84	85	86	87	88	89	90
91	92	93	94	95	96	97	98	99	100

Use the words **10 more** and **10 less** to help you find the numbers.

10 more than 61 is __71__.

10 less than 61 is __51__.

Write the numbers.

1. 10 more than 57 is __67__.

2. 23 is 10 more than ____.

3. 10 less than 89 is ____.

4. 75 is 10 less than ____.

5. 10 more than 34 is ____.

6. 12 is 10 more than ____.

10 More or 10 Less

Use the hundred chart to help.

1	2	3	4	5	6	7	8	9	10
11	12	13	14	15	16	17	18	19	20
21	22	23	24	25	26	27	28	29	30
31	32	33	34	35	36	37	38	39	40
41	42	43	44	45	46	47	48	49	50
51	52	53	54	55	56	57	58	59	60
61	62	63	64	65	66	67	68	69	70
71	72	73	74	75	76	77	78	79	80
81	82	83	84	85	86	87	88	89	90
91	92	93	94	95	96	97	98	99	100

10 More

1. 10 more than 8 is _____.

2. 64 is 10 more than _____.

10 Less

3. 10 less than 22 is _____.

4. 40 is 10 less than _____.

5. Which number is 10 more than 85?

   Ⓐ 95
   Ⓑ 86
   Ⓒ 48
   Ⓓ 15

6. What number is it?
   The number is 10 more than 56.
   It is 10 less than 76.

   Ⓐ 36   Ⓒ 66
   Ⓑ 65   Ⓓ 77

Even and Odd Numbers

An **even** number *can* be shown as two equal parts.
An **odd** number *cannot* be shown as two equal parts.

There are 6 cubes.	There are 7 cubes.
Is 6 an even or odd number?	Is 7 an even or odd number?
Draw lines to match the cubes.	Draw lines to match the cubes.

 The cubes can be shown as two equal parts. 3 + 3 = 6

 The cubes cannot be shown as two equal parts.

6 is an ⚬ⓔⓥⓔⓝ⚬ number.   7 is an ⚬ⓞⓓⓓ⚬ number.

Draw lines to match the cubes. Is the number even or odd?

1.

10 is an _____ number.

2.

9 is an _____ number.

3.

12 is an _____ number.

4.

15 is an _____ number.

5. Write odd or even. Use cubes to help you.
   For an even number, write a doubles fact.

14 _____   17 _____   20 _____

___ + ___ = ___   ___ + ___ = ___   ___ + ___ = ___

Even and Odd Numbers

Circle **even** or **odd.** Use cubes if you need to.
For an even number, write the number sentence.

1. 14
odd (even)

_7_ + _7_ = _14_

2. 13
odd   even

__ + __ = __

3. 18
odd   even

__ + __ = __

4. 19
odd   even

__ + __ = __

5. Draw a picture to solve. Write **even** or **odd.**
Hector has 2 glasses.
He puts 3 ice cubes in one glass
and 2 ice cubes in the other glass.

Does Hector have an odd or even
number of ice cubes?   _____

6. Betty writes a subtraction sentence.
The answer is an even number.
Which subtraction sentence did Betty write?

$8 - 5 = ?$ $7 - 2 = ?$ $9 - 5 = ?$ $6 - 3 = ?$
Ⓐ   Ⓑ   Ⓒ   Ⓓ

7. Algebra Use the drawing to answer the questions.

What number do the cubes show? _____

Is the number even or odd? _____

How do you know? _____

_____

PROBLEM SOLVING

Use Data from a Chart

Use clues to find the secret number on the chart.
Cross out numbers on the chart that do not fit each clue.

Clues:

It is greater than 25.

It is less than 30.

It has a 7 in the ones place.

Cross out the numbers 25 and *less.*

↗1	↗2	↗3	↗4	↗5	↗6	↗7	↗8	↗9	↗0
↗1	↗2	↗3	↗4	↗5	↗6	27	↗8	↗9	↗0
↗1	↗2	↗3	↗4	↗5	↗6	↗7	↗8	↗9	↗0

Cross out the numbers 30 and *greater.*

Cross out the numbers that don't have a 7 in the ones place. 26, 28, 29

The secret number is __27__.

Use the clues to find the secret number.

31	32	33	34	35	36	37	38	39	40
41	42	43	44	45	46	47	48	49	50
51	52	53	54	55	56	57	58	59	60

It is greater than 40. ⟶ Cross out the numbers _____ and less.

It is less than 46. ⟶ Cross out the numbers _____ and greater.

It has a 5 in the ones place. ⟶ Cross out the numbers

_____.

The secret number is _____.

Name _____

Use Data from a Chart

Use clues to find the secret number.
Cross out the numbers on the chart that do not fit the clues.

1. The secret number is an
   even number.
   It is more than 50.
   It has 4 ones.

31	32	33	34	35	36	37	38	39	40
41	42	43	44	45	46	47	48	49	50
51	52	53	54	55	56	57	58	59	60

The secret number is __54__.

2. The secret number has a
   7 in the ones place.
   The tens number is an
   odd number.

61	62	63	64	65	66	67	68	69	70
71	72	73	74	75	76	77	78	79	80
81	82	83	84	85	86	87	88	89	90

The secret number is _____.

Use the clues and the chart to solve the problem.

3. **Reasonableness** The flag that
   Nico waves has an odd number
   in the ones place and an even
   number in the tens place.

   What flag does he wave?

   Ⓐ Red Flag

   Ⓑ Blue Flag

   Ⓒ Yellow Flag

   Ⓓ Green Flag

Numbers on Racing Flags	
Red Flag	25
Blue Flag	14
Yellow Flag	32
Green Flag	6
Orange Flag	17

Name _____

Adding Tens

To add tens, count on by tens.

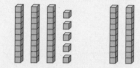

Add: 35 and 20

When you add tens, only the digit in the tens place changes.

Think: Count on 2 tens.

35, 45, 55

So, $35 + 20 = 55$.

Add tens. Use cubes or mental math.

1.

46   and   30 = ___

Count on 3 tens:

46, ___, ___, ___

$46 + 30 =$ ___

2.

34   and   50 = ___

Count on 5 tens:

34, ___, ___, ___, ___, ___

$34 + 50 =$ ___

3.

13 and 40 = ___

Count on 4 tens:

13, ___, ___, ___, ___

$13 + 40 =$ ___

Adding Tens

Add using mental math.

1. $20 + 42 = \underline{62}$

2. $53 + 30 = \underline{\hspace{1cm}}$

3. $50 + 19 = \underline{\hspace{1cm}}$

4. $35 + 40 = \underline{\hspace{1cm}}$

5. $36 + 10 = \underline{\hspace{1cm}}$

47	46	40	37
Ⓐ	Ⓑ	Ⓒ	Ⓓ

6. $21 + 40 = \underline{\hspace{1cm}}$

29	41	60	61
Ⓐ	Ⓑ	Ⓒ	Ⓓ

7. Nellie had 14 rubber bands. Then she bought a pack of 30 rubber bands.

How many rubber bands does Nellie have now?

_____ rubber bands

8. A squirrel has 26 acorns in its nest. It brings 50 more acorns into the nest.

How many acorns does the squirrel have in all?

_____ acorns

9. Spatial Thinking Draw tens and ones to solve.

$69 + 20 = \underline{\hspace{1cm}}$

Name _____

Adding Ones

36 + 7 = _____
Circle the ones to make the next ten.

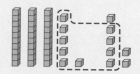

Think: 6 and 4 more make 10.
40 and 3 more make 43.

So, 36 + 7 = 43.

Circle the ones to make the next ten.
Add the ones to the tens.

1.

28 + 4 = _____

2.

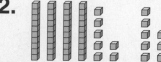

47 + 8 = _____

3.

55 + 7 = _____

4.

36 + 8 = _____

5.

49 + 6 = _____

6.

66 + 8 = _____

Name _____

Adding Ones

Add the ones. Use mental math.

1. $17 + 4 =$ __21__

2. $38 + 5 =$ ____

3. $49 + 3 =$ ____

4. $23 + 2 =$ ____

5. $65 + 7 =$ ____

6. $52 + 8 =$ ____

7. $38 + 9 =$ ____

47	41	31	17
Ⓐ	Ⓑ	Ⓒ	Ⓓ

8. $65 + 6 =$ ____

11	59	61	71
Ⓐ	Ⓑ	Ⓒ	Ⓓ

9. Janna made a necklace using 18 beads.

Leah made a necklace using only 9 beads.

How many beads did the girls use in all?

____ + ____ = ____

____ beads

10. Algebra Find the missing number that
will make the next ten.

$53 +$ ____ $= 60$

6	7	8	9
Ⓐ	Ⓑ	Ⓒ	Ⓓ

Adding Tens and Ones

Find 25 + 34.

25 and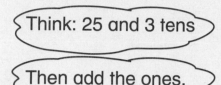

First, count on by tens to add the tens:

Think: 25 and 3 tens

Then add the ones.

25, 35, 45, 55

55 and 4 ones is 59.

So, 25 + 34 = 59.

Add. Use mental math or cubes.

1. 34 + 23

34 and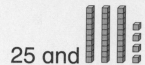

34, _____, _____

54 and _____ ones is _____.

So, 34 + 23 = _____.

2. 52 + 33

52 and

52, _____, _____, _____

_____ and _____ ones is _____.

So, 52 + 33 = _____.

3. 42 + 12 = _____

4. 25 + 21 = _____

Name _____

Adding Tens and Ones

Add using mental math.

1. 41 + 24 = 65

2. 53 + 15 = _____

3. 56 + 33 = _____

4. 62 + 25 = _____

5. 43 + 36 = _____

6. 50 + 25 = _____

7. 37 + 21 = _____

8. 17 + 52 = _____

9. 46 + 32 = _____

68	70	74	78
Ⓐ	Ⓑ	Ⓒ	Ⓓ

10. 61 + 13 = _____

78	74	70	63
Ⓐ	Ⓑ	Ⓒ	Ⓓ

11. Tad has 72 seashells. He finds 15 more shells.

How many seashells does Tad have in all?

82	83	87	92
Ⓐ	Ⓑ	Ⓒ	Ⓓ

12. Estimation One bunch has 31 grapes.
Another bunch has 28 grapes.
About how many grapes are there in all?

Ⓐ about 30 grapes   Ⓒ about 60 grapes

Ⓑ about 50 grapes   Ⓓ about 70 grapes

Name _____

Adding on a Hundred Chart

Find 16 + 23.

1	2	3	4	5	6	7	8	9	10
11	12	13	14	15	16	17	18	19	20
21	22	23	24	25	26	27	28	29	30
31	32	33	34	35	36	37	38	39	40
41	42	43	44	45	46	47	48	49	50
51	52	53	54	55	56	57	58	59	60
61	62	63	64	65	66	67	68	69	70
71	72	73	74	75	76	77	78	79	80
81	82	83	84	85	86	87	88	89	90
91	92	93	94	95	96	97	98	99	100

1. Start on square 16.

2. Move down 2 rows to show the tens in 23.

3. Move 3 squares to the right to show the ones in 23.

4. Where did you stop? _39_

So, _16_ + _23_ = _39_.

Add using the hundred chart.

1. 12 + 11 = ____   **2.** 31 + 45 = ____

3. 81 + 14 = ____   **4.** 48 + 51 = ____

5. 24 + 23 = ____   **6.** 33 + 56 = ____

7. 52 + 15 = ____   **8.** 15 + 14 = ____

9. Number Sense Write the number of tens in each number.

67 ____ tens   85 ____ tens   94 ____ tens

R 6·4

Name _____

Adding on a Hundred Chart

Add using the
hundred chart.

1. 47 + 31 = _78_

2. 18 + 25 = ____

3. 28 + 43 = ____

4. 37 + 56 = ____

1	2	3	4	5	6	7	8	9	10
11	12	13	14	15	16	17	18	19	20
21	22	23	24	25	26	27	28	29	30
31	32	33	34	35	36	37	38	39	40
41	42	43	44	45	46	47	48	49	50
51	52	53	54	55	56	57	58	59	60
61	62	63	64	65	66	67	68	69	70
71	72	73	74	75	76	77	78	79	80
81	82	83	84	85	86	87	88	89	90
91	92	93	94	95	96	97	98	99	100

5. 35 + 28 = ____

65   63   62   60
Ⓐ   Ⓑ   Ⓒ   Ⓓ

6. 64 + 26 = ____

80   82   90   92
Ⓐ   Ⓑ   Ⓒ   Ⓓ

7. Geometry Choose the shapes that answer the question.
What weights can you put on the scale to make it balance?

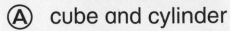
Ⓐ cube and cylinder   Ⓒ rectangular prism and cube

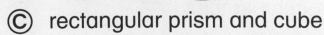
Ⓑ sphere and cube   Ⓓ rectangular prism and sphere

P 6•4

Adding Multiples of 10

Find 40 + 20.

1. Start on square 40.

2. Count on 2 tens by moving down 2 rows in the 10's column.

1	2	3	4	5	6	7	8	9	10
11	12	13	14	15	16	17	18	19	20
21	22	23	24	25	26	27	28	29	30
31	32	33	34	35	36	37	38	39	40
41	42	43	44	45	46	47	48	49	50
51	52	53	54	55	56	57	58	59	60
61	62	63	64	65	66	67	68	69	70
71	72	73	74	75	76	77	78	79	80
81	82	83	84	85	86	87	88	89	90
91	92	93	94	95	96	97	98	99	100

3. Where did you stop? _60_

So, _40_ + _20_ = _60_.

Add using the hundred chart.

1. 30 + 20 = _____

2. 40 + 30 = _____

3. 50 + 10 = _____

4. 30 + 30 = _____

5. 20 + 70 = _____

6. 50 + 40 = _____

7. 10 + 30 = _____

8. 40 + 40 = _____

9. **Number Sense** Write the number of tens in each number.

34 _____ tens   57 _____ tens   82 _____ tens

Adding Multiples of 10

Add using the
hundred chart.

1	2	3	4	5	6	7	8	9	10
11	12	13	14	15	16	17	18	19	20
21	22	23	24	25	26	27	28	29	30
31	32	33	34	35	36	37	38	39	40
41	42	43	44	45	46	47	48	49	50
51	52	53	54	55	56	57	58	59	60
61	62	63	64	65	66	67	68	69	70
71	72	73	74	75	76	77	78	79	80
81	82	83	84	85	86	87	88	89	90
91	92	93	94	95	96	97	98	99	100

1. 50 + 30 = 80

2. 20 + 30 = ____

3. 20 + 50 = ____

4. 40 + 60 = ____

5. 40 + 30 = ____

70   60   50   40
Ⓐ   Ⓑ   Ⓒ   Ⓓ

6. 60 + 30 = ____

40   70   80   90
Ⓐ   Ⓑ   Ⓒ   Ⓓ

7. A year ago, Ray's puppy
weighed 10 pounds.
Now his puppy weighs
30 pounds more.
How much does Ray's
puppy weigh now?

_____

_____

Name _____

Problem Solving: Look for a Pattern

Look for a pattern in these rows of buttons.
Draw buttons to finish the pattern.

2

4

6

_8_

The pattern is to add __2__ buttons each time.

Look for a pattern. Solve.

1. Emma is collecting cans for a recycling project. The chart shows how many cans she plans to collect each week. What is the pattern?

_____ more cans each week

Week 1	10 cans
Week 2	20 cans
Week 3	30 cans
Week 4	? cans
Week 5	? cans

2. What is Emma's goal for week 4 and week 5?

Week 4:_____   Week 5: _____

3. **Journal** On a separate piece of paper, create a pattern problem for a friend to solve. Draw a picture or write a story problem.

Problem Solving: Look for a Pattern

Finish the pattern. Solve.

1. On Monday, a cook has 65 frozen pizzas. Each day she bakes 10 of the pizzas. Tuesday, she has 55 pizzas left. Wednesday, she has 45 pizzas left. Continue the pattern.

Monday	65
Tuesday	55
Wednesday	45
Thursday	35
Friday	25

What is the pattern?

Ⓐ Add 5.

Ⓑ Add 10.

Ⓒ Subtract 5.

Ⓓ Subtract 10.

2. In Week 1, Cleo picked 2 tomatoes. In Week 2, she picked 7 tomatoes. In Week 3, she picked 12 tomatoes. Continue the pattern.

Week 1	2
Week 2	7
Week 3	12
Week 4	
Week 5	

What is the pattern?

Ⓐ Add 5.

Ⓑ Add 7.

Ⓒ Subtract 5.

Ⓓ Subtract 7.

3. Journal Patty made 4 headbands last week. She made 8 this week. Next week, she will make 12. What is the pattern? How many headbands will Patty make the following week?

_____ _____ headbands

Subtracting Tens

Here are two ways you can find 57 − 30.

1. Count back 3 tens, or 30.

57, 47, 37, 27

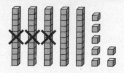

When you subtract tens, only the tens digit changes.

2. Use cubes to subtract the tens.

50 − 30 = 20

Then subtract the ones.

7 − 0 = 7

So, 57 − 30 = 27.

Count back to subtract tens. Use cubes if needed.

1. 64 − 30 =

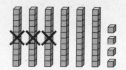

64, _____, _____, _____

64 − 30 = _____

2. 62 − 40 = _____

3. 76 − 20 = _____

4. 84 − 50 = _____

5. 95 − 70 = _____

Subtracting Tens

Subtract. Use mental math.

1. 76 − 40 = 36

2. 98 − 50 = ____

3. 94 − 60 = ____

4. 33 − 20 = ____

5. 65 − 10 = ____

6. 52 − 30 = ____

7. 47 − 30 = ____

Ⓐ 37

Ⓑ 30

Ⓒ 20

Ⓓ 17

8. 61 − 40 = ____

Ⓐ 20

Ⓑ 21

Ⓒ 30

Ⓓ 41

9. Use mental math to solve.

A box holds 48 crackers. Austin ate 10 of them.

How many crackers are left in the box?

Ⓐ 18

Ⓑ 28

Ⓒ 38

Ⓓ 58

10. Number Sense Allie had 36 dolls. On Thursday she gave 10 dolls away, and on Friday she gave away 10 more.

How many dolls does she have now?

Ⓐ 46

Ⓑ 36

Ⓒ 26

Ⓓ 16

Finding Parts of 100

Find parts for 100.
Draw more tens to make 100.

Think: Add on to make 100.

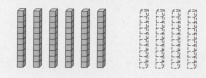

60 and __40__ is 100.

60 + __40__ = 100

Now draw tens and ones to make 100. Add on.

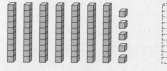

75 and __25__ is 100.

75 + __25__ = 100

Draw tens to find the other part of 100.

1.

50 and _____ is 100.

50 + _____ = 100

....

Draw tens and ones to make 100. Add on.

2.

45 and _____ is 100.

45 + _____ = 100

Finding Parts of 100

Add on to find the other part of 100.

1. $54 + \underline{46} = 100$

2. $29 + \underline{} = 100$

3. $43 + \underline{} = 100$

4. $72 + \underline{} = 100$

5. $89 + \underline{} = 100$

6. $18 + \underline{} = 100$

7. $37 + \underline{} = 100$

8. $61 + \underline{} = 100$

9. $65 + \underline{} = 100$

10. $46 + \underline{} = 100$

Solve.

11. Latisha had a box of 100 birthday cards. So far, she has sent out 47 cards.

    How many cards are left in the box?

    Ⓐ 51 cards

    Ⓑ 52 cards

    Ⓒ 53 cards

    Ⓓ 54 cards

12. **Reasonableness** Do not add or subtract. Read each answer. Choose the most reasonable answer.

    A store had 100 class rings. They sold 37 rings. How many are left?

    Ⓐ 63 rings

    Ⓑ 50 rings

    Ⓒ 35 rings

    Ⓓ 10 rings

Subtracting on a Hundred Chart

A hundred chart can help you subtract.

Find 36 − 24.

I	2	3	4	5	6	7	8	9	10
11	12	13	14	15	16	17	18	19	20
21	22	23	24	25	26	27	28	29	30
31	32	33	34	35	36	37	38	39	40
41	42	43	44	45	46	47	48	49	50
51	52	53	54	55	56	57	58	59	60
61	62	63	64	65	66	67	68	69	70
71	72	73	74	75	76	77	78	79	80
81	82	83	84	85	86	87	88	89	90
91	92	93	94	95	96	97	98	99	100

1. Start at 24.

2. Move down to 34.
   This is the row that 36 is in.

   One row down makes __10__.

3. Move right from 34 to 36 to count __2__ ones.

4. Count the tens down and ones across.

   __10__ + __2__ = __12__ , so 36 − 24 = 12.

Subtract using the hundred chart.

1. 87 − 72 = _____

2. 79 − 48 = _____

3. 65 − 41 = _____

4. 99 − 52 = _____

5. 35 − 13 = _____

6. 84 − 33 = _____

Subtracting on a Hundred Chart

Subtract using the hundred chart.

1	2	3	4	5	6	7	8	9	10
11	12	13	14	15	16	17	18	19	20
21	22	23	24	25	26	27	28	29	30
31	32	33	34	35	36	37	38	39	40
41	42	43	44	45	46	47	48	49	50
51	52	53	54	55	56	57	58	59	60
61	62	63	64	65	66	67	68	69	70
71	72	73	74	75	76	77	78	79	80
81	82	83	84	85	86	87	88	89	90
91	92	93	94	95	96	97	98	99	100

1. $47 - 31 =$ ___16___

2. $78 - 25 =$ _____

3. $99 - 43 =$ _____

4. $37 - 16 =$ _____

5. $55 - 23 =$ _____

6. $64 - 26 =$ _____

7. A pan holds 36 biscuits. Kiana put 12 biscuits on the pan.

How many more biscuits will fit on the pan?

Ⓐ 24 biscuits

Ⓑ 23 biscuits

Ⓒ 22 biscuits

Ⓓ 21 biscuits

8. A garden has room for 22 flowers. Dan needs to plant 11 more flowers.

How many flowers did Dan already plant?

Ⓐ 10 flowers

Ⓑ 11 flowers

Ⓒ 12 flowers

Ⓓ 13 flowers

9. Journal Explain how to use a hundred chart to subtract.

_____

_____

Subtracting Multiples of 10

A hundred chart can help you subtract.

Find 60 − 30.

1	2	3	4	5	6	7	8	9	10
11	12	13	14	15	16	17	18	19	20
21	22	23	24	25	26	27	28	29	30
31	32	33	34	35	36	37	38	39	40
41	42	43	44	45	46	47	48	49	50
51	52	53	54	55	56	57	58	59	60
61	62	63	64	65	66	67	68	69	70
71	72	73	74	75	76	77	78	79	80
81	82	83	84	85	86	87	88	89	90
91	92	93	94	95	96	97	98	99	100

1. Start at 60.

2. Move back by ten from 60 to 50, from 50 to 40, and from 40 to 30. 30 is the difference.

   One row up makes __10__.

3. Count the tens up.

   __30__, so 60 − 30 = 30.

Subtract using the hundred chart.

1. 70 − 10 = _____

2. 90 − 10 = _____

3. 40 − 10 = _____

4. 80 − 40 = _____

5. 50 − 30 = _____

6. 60 − 20 = _____

Subtracting Multiples of 10

Subtract using the hundred chart.

1. 50 − 30 = _20_

1	2	3	4	5	6	7	8	9	10
11	12	13	14	15	16	17	18	19	20
21	22	23	24	25	26	27	28	29	30
31	32	33	34	35	36	37	38	39	40
41	42	43	44	45	46	47	48	49	50
51	52	53	54	55	56	57	58	59	60
61	62	63	64	65	66	67	68	69	70
71	72	73	74	75	76	77	78	79	80
81	82	83	84	85	86	87	88	89	90
91	92	93	94	95	96	97	98	99	100

2. 80 − 30 = _____

3. 90 − 40 = _____

4. 40 − 20 = _____

5. 60 − 20 = _____

6. 70 − 10 = _____

7. A pan holds 40 biscuits. Kiana put 10 biscuits on the pan.

How many more biscuits will fit on the pan?

Ⓐ 30 biscuits

Ⓑ 20 biscuits

Ⓒ 10 biscuits

Ⓓ 40 biscuits

8. A garden has room for 90 flowers. Dan needs to plant 50 more flowers.

How many flowers did Dan already plant?

Ⓐ 30 flowers

Ⓑ 40 flowers

Ⓒ 10 flowers

Ⓓ 20 flowers

9. Journal Explain how to use a hundred chart to subtract.

_____

_____

Problem Solving: Missing or Extra Information

Solve.

There are 4 children
on a bowling team.
Mike bowls a score of 55.
Sherry bowls a score of 30.
How much higher is Mike's score?

Sometimes you do not have enough information to solve a problem. Sometimes you have too much information and you do not need it to solve a problem.

1. What do you need to find out?

The difference between Mike's and Sherry's score.

2. What information do you need to solve the problem?

Mike's score and Sherry's score:

$$55 - 30 = 25$$

3. What information is extra?

There are 4 children on the team.

Cross out the extra information.
Solve the problem if you have the information you need.

1. There are 39 adults at the bowling alley.
There are 9 children at the bowling alley.
Mark bowls a score of 82.

How many more adults than children are there?

Solve if you can: _____ − _____ = _____

Problem Solving: Missing or Extra Information

Circle **Extra Information** or **Missing Information**.
Then write a number sentence if the problem can be solved.

1. Julia painted 12 pictures and made 3 clay baskets at school. Julia took 5 pictures home. How many pictures are left at school?

(Extra Information)

Missing Information

12 – 5 = 7 pictures

2. Nico cut out 15 red circles and 10 yellow circles. Then he gave away some red circles. How many red circles does Nico have left?

Extra Information

Missing Information

____ – ____ = ____ red circles

Spatial Thinking Draw a picture to solve each problem. Then choose the correct answer.

3. A bush had 18 berries. A raccoon ate 9 of the berries. Then the raccoon ate 6 fish. How many berries are left?

Ⓐ 11 berries
Ⓑ 10 berries
Ⓒ 9 berries
Ⓓ 8 berries

4. A bowl holds 16 oranges and 4 apples. Children eat 9 oranges. How many oranges are left in the bowl?

Ⓐ 7 oranges
Ⓑ 8 oranges
Ⓒ 9 oranges
Ⓓ 10 oranges

Regrouping 10 Ones for 1 Ten

Find the sum.

24 + 8 = _____

Regroup 10 ones as 1 ten.

There are __3__ tens and __2__ ones

24 + 8 = _32_

Tens	Ones

Regroup 10 ones as 1 ten.
Add. Count the tens and the ones.

1.

Tens	Ones

28 + 3 = _____

2.

Tens	Ones

47 + 7 = _____

3.

Tens	Ones

55 + 6 = _____

4.

Tens	Ones

36 + 8 = _____

R 8·1

Name _____

Regrouping 10 Ones for 1 Ten

Use cubes and a workmat.
Add. Regroup if you need to.

Show.	Add.	Do you need to regroup?		Show.
1. 24	7	(Yes)	No	$24 + 7 = \underline{31}$
2. 56	9	Yes	No	$56 + 9 = \underline{\hphantom{00}}$
3. 92	6	Yes	No	$92 + 6 = \underline{\hphantom{00}}$

4. Pat had 6 forks. Then she bought a pack of 18 forks. How many forks does she have now?

Ⓐ 12
Ⓑ 14
Ⓒ 24
Ⓓ 26

5. Theo counted 69 red plates. Then he counted 8 blue plates. How many plates did he count in all?

Ⓐ 79
Ⓑ 77
Ⓒ 71
Ⓓ 61

6. Spatial Thinking Solve the problem by drawing tens and ones in the place-value chart.

$48 + 5 = \underline{\hphantom{00}}$

Tens	Ones

Name _____

Models to Add Two- and One-Digit Numbers

Add 35 + 7.

Step 1:
How many ones?

5 + 7 = _12_

Tens	Ones

Tens	Ones
□	
3	5
+	7
	2

Step 2:
Regroup 12 as
1 ten and 2 ones.
Write 2 ones.

Tens	Ones

Tens	Ones
1	
3	5
+	7
	2

Step 3:
How many tens?

3 + 1 = _4_ tens

Tens	Ones

Tens	Ones
1	
3	5
+	7
4	2

So, 35 + 7 = _42_.

Use connecting cubes and the workmat. Add.
Did you need to regroup? Circle **yes** or **no.**

Tens	Ones
□	
4	6
+	9

Yes   No

Tens	Ones
□	
5	2
+	7

Yes   No

Tens	Ones
□	
3	8
+	5

Yes   No

Tens	Ones
□	
6	7
+	3

Yes   No

Models to Add Two- and One-Digit Numbers

Use connecting cubes and a workmat. Add.
Do you need to regroup? Circle **Yes** or **No**.

1.

Tens	Ones
1	
2	8
+	5
3	3

(Yes)   No

2.

Tens	Ones
6	4
+	9

Yes   No

3.

Tens	Ones
5	2
+	5

Yes   No

4.

Tens	Ones
	7
+ 1	9

Yes   No

5.

Tens	Ones
2	5
+	7

Yes   No

6.

Tens	Ones
4	3
+	8

Yes   No

7.

Tens	Ones
5	4
+	2

Yes   No

8.

Tens	Ones
3	3
+	7

Yes   No

9. A crow ate 22 kernels of corn. Then it ate 4 more kernels. How many kernels did it eat in all?

Ⓐ 18 kernels

Ⓑ 20 kernels

Ⓒ 24 kernels

Ⓓ 26 kernels

10. Algebra Write the missing numbers in the boxes.

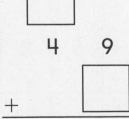

Name _____

Adding Two- and One-Digit Numbers

Remember the steps for adding.
Step 1: Add the ones.
Step 2: Regroup if there are more than 10 ones.
Step 3: Add the tens.

$37 + 6 = ?$
There are more than 10 ones.
Regroup 13 as 1 ten and 3 ones. Add.

Tens	Ones
1	
3	7
+	6
4	3

Use paper and pencil to add.

1. Do you need to regroup?
Yes   No

Tens	Ones
2	8
+	4

2. Do you need to regroup?
Yes   No

Tens	Ones
3	6
+	9

3. Do you need to regroup?
Yes   No

Tens	Ones
3	4
+	5

4. Do you need to regroup?
Yes   No

Tens	Ones
4	6
+	4

Adding Two- and One-Digit Numbers

Add. Regroup if you need to.

1.

Tens	Ones
I	
7	6
+	7
8	3

2.

Tens	Ones
6	4
+	3

3.

Tens	Ones
8	3
+	6

4.

Tens	Ones
3	7
+	9

5.

Tens	Ones
7	5
+	7

6.

Tens	Ones
5	0
+	8

7.

Tens	Ones
7	6
+	4

8.

Tens	Ones
8	3
+	5

9. Bessie has 25 flowers. Then she picks 9 more flowers. How many flowers does Bessie have in all?

(A) 33

(B) 34

(C) 35

(D) 36

10. Journal Tell how you know when to regroup.

_____

_____

_____

_____

Models to Add Two-Digit Numbers

Add 46 + 18.

Step 1:
How many ones?

$6 + 8 =$ __14__

Tens	Ones

Tens	Ones
4	6
+ 1	8
	4

Step 2:
Do I need to regroup?

(yes)   no

Tens	Ones

Tens	Ones
1	
4	6
+ 1	8
	4

Step 3:
How many tens?

$5 + 1 =$ __6__ tens

Tens	Ones

Tens	Ones
1	
4	6
+ 1	8
6	4

So, 46 + 18 = __64__.

Follow the steps. Use connecting cubes and the workmat. Add.

1.

Tens	Ones
2	4
+ 2	9

Tens	Ones
5	2
+ 1	7

Tens	Ones
3	8
+ 4	5

Tens	Ones
1	7
+ 6	3

Name _____

Models to Add Two-Digit Numbers

Use connecting cubes and the workmat. Add.
Do you need to regroup? Circle **Yes** or **No**.

1.
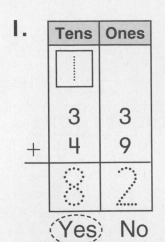

Tens	Ones
3	3
+ 4	9
8	2

Yes No

2.

Tens	Ones
5	1
+ 4	7

Yes No

3.
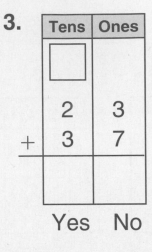

Tens	Ones
2	3
+ 3	7

Yes No

4.

Tens	Ones
4	4
+ 2	8

Yes No

---

5. Lia counts 38 red paper cups and 25 blue paper cups. How many paper cups did she count in all?

Ⓐ 13

Ⓑ 43

Ⓒ 53

Ⓓ 63

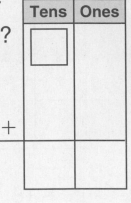

Tens	Ones
+	

---

6. Reasonableness Use the clues to solve the riddle.
I am between 24 and 34.
You say my name when you count by twos from zero.
You say my name when you count by fives from zero.
What number am I?

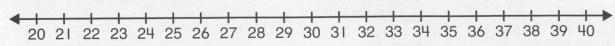

20 21 22 23 24 25 26 27 28 29 30 31 32 33 34 35 36 37 38 39 40

I am the number _____.

Adding Two-Digit Numbers

Remember the steps for adding:

Step 1: Add the ones.   **Step 2:** Regroup if you need to.   **Step 3:** Add the tens.

$34 + 27 = ?$
Regroup 11 ones as 1 ten and 1 one.

Tens	Ones
[1]	
3	4
+ 2	7
6	1

$12 + 36 = ?$
You do not need to regroup 8 ones.

Tens	Ones
[ ]	[ ]
1	2
+ 3	6
4	8

Write the addition problem. Find the sum.

1.

$15 + 26$

Tens	Ones
[ ]	
1	5
+ 2	6

$32 + 24$

Tens	Ones
[ ]	
3	2
+ 2	

$28 + 15$

Tens	Ones
[ ]	
2	8
+	

$49 + 13$

Tens	Ones
[ ]	
+	

2. **Algebra** Begin with 39. Find the number that gives you a sum of 56. Use connecting cubes to help.

The number is _____.

Tens	Ones
[ ]	
3	9
+	
5	6

Adding Two-Digit Numbers

Write the addition problem. Find the sum.

1. 26 + 52

Tens	Ones
2	6
+ 5	2
7	8

2. 31 + 19

Tens	Ones
+	

3. 47 + 28

Tens	Ones
+	

4. 56 + 34

Tens	Ones
+	

5. 63 + 26

Tens	Ones
+	

6. 75 + 13

Tens	Ones
+	

7. 68 + 29

Tens	Ones
+	

8. 54 + 37

Tens	Ones
+	

9. Paul has a stack of 43 pennies and a stack of 36 pennies. How many pennies does he have altogether?

Ⓐ 47 pennies

Ⓑ 66 pennies

Ⓒ 79 pennies

Ⓓ 89 pennies

10. Estimation One jar has 38 buttons. Another jar has 43 buttons. About how many buttons are in both jars?

Ⓐ about 80 buttons

Ⓑ about 70 buttons

Ⓒ about 60 buttons

Ⓓ about 50 buttons

Adding on a Number Line

You can show addition on a number line.

$10 + 29 =$ _____

Start at 0. Move 10 spaces to the right.

Start at 10. Move 29 spaces to the right.

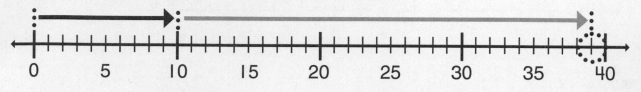

$10 + 29 = \underline{39}$

I. Show $24 + 7$ on the number line.

$24 + 7 =$ _____

2. Journal Write an addition sentence. Explain how to show it on a number line.

_____ + _____ = _____

_____

_____

Adding on a Number Line

1. Show the addition problem on the number line.

18 + 23 = _____

2. What addition problem does the number line show?

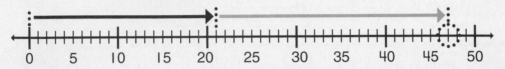

_____ + _____ = _____

3. Journal A class has 19 girls and 19 boys. How many girls and boys all together are in the class? Draw a number line to solve. Explain why you don't begin at 0 to show the second number.

_____

_____

_____

Adding More than Two Numbers

You can add three or four numbers in any order.
Remember to add the ones first.

Look for doubles.

$$
\begin{array}{r}
14 \\
35 \\
+\ 24 \\
\hline
73
\end{array}
$$

$4 + 4 = 8$
$8 + 5 = 13$

Make a ten.

$$
\begin{array}{r}
13 \\
26 \\
24 \\
+\ 12 \\
\hline
75
\end{array}
$$

$6 + 4 = 10$
$3 + 2 = 5$
$10 + 5 = 15$

Count on.

$$
\begin{array}{r}
53 \\
19 \\
+\ 22 \\
\hline
94
\end{array}
$$

Add 9 and 3.
$9 + 3 = 12$
Count on from 12. 13, 14.

Add. Circle the numbers you add first.

1. Look for doubles.	2. Count on.	3. Make a ten.	4. Choose a way to add.
21			
10	12	15	26
34	17	28	22
+ 24	+ 24	+ 22	+ 36

5. Journal Write an addition problem with three or four
numbers. Solve it. Then have a friend solve it. Compare
how you and your friend add the numbers.

Adding More than Two Numbers

Add. Circle the two numbers you added first.

I.   34
      19
  + 41
    94

2.   61
      10
  + 26

3.   28
      34
      12
  + 5

4.   31
      19
      21
  + 26

5.   47
      22
  + 24

6.   51
       8
  + 25

7.   52
      14
       8
  + 24

8.   23
       4
      41
  + 18

---

9. These animals live in a big garden:

   37 snails

   49 worms

   12 moths

   How many animals live in the garden in all?

   Ⓐ   98

   Ⓑ   97

   Ⓒ   88

   Ⓓ   87

10. **Number Sense** Use the numbers shown. Make the sum of the numbers across equal the sum of the numbers down.

   7   5   1   9   3

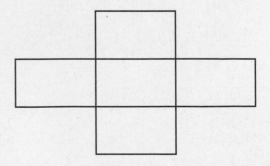

Ways to Add

Use **mental math** to add.
43 + 20
Count up by tens. 43, 53, 63.

43 + 20 = 63

Use **cubes** to add.
27 + 18
Regroup 10 ones for one ten.

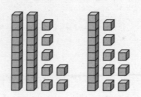

27 + 18 = 45

Use **paper and pencil** to add.
45 + 15

$$\begin{array}{r} 45 \\ + 15 \\ \hline 0 \end{array}$$

Write 1 ten over the tens column.

45 + 15 = 60

Use a **calculator** to add.
56 + 29

| 5 | 6 | + | 2 | 9 |

56 + 29 = 85

Circle how you will solve the problem. Then add.

1. mental math
cubes
paper and pencil
calculator

34 + 23 = 57

2. mental math
cubes
paper and pencil
calculator

46 + 30 = ____

3. mental math
cubes
paper and pencil
calculator

54 + 17 = ____

4. mental math
cubes
paper and pencil
calculator

73 + 18 = ____

Ways to Add

Circle how you will solve the problem. Then add.

1.   5 6
   + 3 8   mental math
   9 4
            (paper and pencil)

2.   3 5
   + 2 4   mental math

            paper and pencil

Write the way you will solve the problem.
Then add and write the sum.

3. 61 + 13 = _____

_____

4. 28 + 38 = _____

_____

5. Damien has 48 red marbles. He has 39 blue marbles.
How many marbles does he have in all?

    71   77   79   87
    Ⓐ   Ⓑ   Ⓒ   Ⓓ

How did you solve the problem?

Ⓐ mental math   Ⓒ paper and pencil

Ⓑ calculator   Ⓓ cubes

6. Number Sense Write a problem that you
would solve with a calculator. Explain why.
Then use a calculator to find the answer.

_____ + _____ = _____

_____

Name _____

Problem Solving: Draw a Picture and Write a Number Sentence

Look for clue words to help you solve a story problem.

Tina has 23 counters.
She gets 27 more counters.
How many counters does Tina have in all?

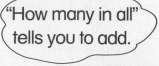
"How many in all" tells you to add.

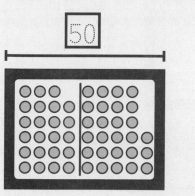

$23 + 27 = 50$

Tens	Ones
⬚ 1	
2	3
+ 2	7
5	0

Draw pictures to solve the problem.
Then write a number sentence.

I. Raul has 15 counters.
He gets 19 more counters.
How many does he have in all?

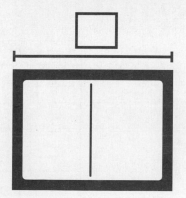

___ + ___ = ___

Tens	Ones
⬚	
+	

Name _____

Problem Solving: Draw a Picture and Write a Number Sentence

Write a number sentence to solve each problem.
Use the part-part-whole mat if needed.

1. Jordan had 19 yo-yos. Then he got 17 more. How many yo-yos does he have now?

   $\underline{19} + \underline{17} = \underline{36}$ yo-yos

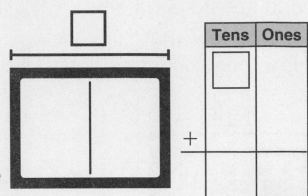

2. There are 32 crayons. 14 crayons are yellow and the rest are green. How many crayons are green?

   _____ + _____ = _____ toys

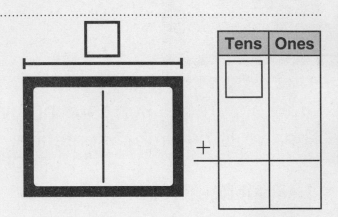

3. Curt made paper cranes. He made 45 blue cranes. He made 17 green cranes.

   Which number sentence shows how many paper cranes he made in all?

   Ⓐ $45 - 17 = 28$

   Ⓑ $17 + 17 = 34$

   Ⓒ $45 + 17 = 62$

   Ⓓ $45 + 45 = 90$

4. **Algebra** Which number is missing?

   Ⓐ 4

   Ⓑ 3

   Ⓒ 2

   Ⓓ 1

Tens	Ones
1	
2	8
+	1	4
?	2

Regrouping 1 Ten for 10 Ones

Subtract 7 from 42.

Show 42.

Tens	Ones

There are not enough ones to subtract 7.

Regroup.

Tens	Ones

1 ten becomes 10 ones.

Subtract 7 ones.

Tens	Ones

Do you need to regroup?

(Yes)   No

$12 - 7 = 5$ ones

$42 - 7 = \underline{35}$

Subtract. Regroup if needed.
Use cubes and a workmat to help.

1. Subtract 5 from 31.

Show 31.

Tens	Ones

Regroup.

Tens	Ones

Subtract __5__ ones.

Tens	Ones

Do you need to regroup?

(Yes)   No

$11 - 5 = \underline{6}$ ones.

$31 - 5 = \underline{}$

R 9·1

Name _____

Regrouping 1 Ten for 10 Ones

Subtract. Regroup if you need to.
Use cubes and a workmat to help.

Show.	Subtract.	Do you need to regroup?	Find the difference.
1. 47	9	(Yes) No	$47 - 9 =$ 38
2. 52	6	Yes No	$52 - 6 =$ ____
3. 38	5	Yes No	$38 - 5 =$ ____

4. Use cubes and a workmat to solve the problem.

An old building has 48 windows. 9 of them are broken. How many windows are not broken?

Ⓐ 39 windows

Ⓑ 40 windows

Ⓒ 41 windows

Ⓓ 42 windows

5. Spatial Thinking The pole is 30 feet tall. The bug has crawled 14 feet. How much farther does the bug need to crawl to get to the top?

It needs to crawl

____ feet farther.

Models to Subtract Two- and One-Digit Numbers

Subtract 8 from 52.

Step 1	Step 2	Step 3
Think: There are not enough ones to subtract 8.	Regroup 1 ten as 10 ones. Write 12 ones. $12 - 8 = 4$ ones	Subtract the tens. $4 - 0 = 4$ tens

Step 1

Tens	Ones

Tens	Ones
5	2
−	8

Step 2

Tens	Ones

Tens	Ones
4	12
5	2
−	8
	4

Step 3

Tens	Ones

Tens	Ones
4	12
5	2
−	8
4	4

So, $52 - 8 = \underline{44}$.

Subtract. Use cubes and a workmat to help.
Did you need to regroup? Circle **yes** or **no**.

1.

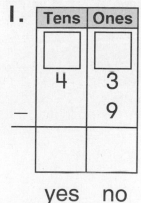

Tens	Ones
4	3
−	9

yes   no

Tens	Ones
6	9
−	3

yes   no

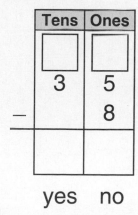

Tens	Ones
3	5
−	8

yes   no

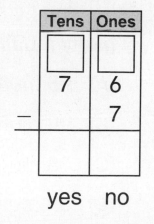

Tens	Ones
7	6
−	7

yes   no

Models to Subtract Two- and One-Digit Numbers

Subtract. Regroup if you need to.
Use cubes and a workmat to help.

1.

Tens	Ones
1	16
2	6
−	7
1	9

2.

Tens	Ones
5	2
−	8

3.

Tens	Ones
7	7
−	5

4.

Tens	Ones
3	9
−	6

5.

Tens	Ones
4	5
−	7

6.

Tens	Ones
6	1
−	7

7.

Tens	Ones
9	0
−	4

8.

Tens	Ones
6	8
−	9

9. Solve.

A bakery makes 64 muffins. They sell 29 muffins by noon. How many muffins are left?

Ⓐ 45 muffins

Ⓑ 44 muffins

Ⓒ 35 muffins

Ⓓ 34 muffins

10. Reasonableness There are 45 children in the gym. Some children leave. How many children could be in the gym now?

Ⓐ 37 children

Ⓑ 45 children

Ⓒ 51 children

Ⓓ 62 children

Subtracting Two- and One-Digit Numbers

Remember the steps for subtracting.

Step 1
Think: Are there enough ones to subtract?

Step 2
Regroup the ones if you need to. Subtract.

Step 3
Subtract the tens.

Subtract.
Regroup if you need to.

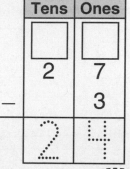

Tens	Ones
2	7
−	3
2	4

Regroup?   Yes   (No)

Tens	Ones
3	12
4̶	2̶
−	6
3	6

Regroup?   (Yes)   No

Remember the steps for subtracting.
Subtract. Regroup if you need to.

1.

Tens	Ones
2	5
−	4

Tens	Ones
4	1
−	8

Tens	Ones
6	5
−	7

Tens	Ones
7	8
−	9

2. Journal Write a subtraction problem that needs regrouping.

Tens	Ones
−	

Subtracting Two- and One-Digit Numbers

Subtract. Regroup if you need to.

1.

Tens	Ones
6	12
7	2
−	5
6	7

2.

Tens	Ones
6	1
−	7

3.

Tens	Ones
8	3
−	6

4.

Tens	Ones
3	8
−	3

5.

Tens	Ones
7	6
−	2

6.

Tens	Ones
9	3
−	4

7.

Tens	Ones
2	6
−	7

8.

Tens	Ones
8	7
−	8

9. Katara takes 21 kites to the park. She sells 9 of the kites. How many kites are left?

(A) 3 kites

(B) 11 kites

(C) 12 kites

(D) 30 kites

10. Journal Tell how you know when to regroup.

_____

_____

_____

_____

_____

Models to Subtract Two-Digit Numbers

Subtract 16 from 43.

Step 1	**Step 2**	**Step 3**
Think: There are not enough ones to subtract 6.	Think: Do I need to regroup?	Think: Subtract the tens.

$$13 - 6 = \underline{7} \text{ ones} \quad 3 - 1 = \underline{2} \text{ tens}$$

Tens	Ones
▮▮▮▮	▫ ▫ ▫

Tens	Ones
▮▮▮	(regrouped ones)

Tens	Ones
▮▮	▫ ▫ / ▫ ▫ / ▫ ✕✕ / ▫ ✕✕ / ▫ ✕✕

Tens	Ones
4	3
− 1	6

Tens	Ones
3	13
4̶	3̶
− 1	6
	7

Tens	Ones
3	13
4̶	3̶
− 1	6
2	7

So, $43 - 16 = \underline{27}$.

Subtract. Regroup if you need to.
Use cubes and a workmat.

1.

Tens	Ones
3	7
− 1	5

Tens	Ones
5	0
− 1	3

Tens	Ones
7	6
− 2	8

Tens	Ones
4	5
− 2	7

Name _____

Models to Subtract Two-Digit Numbers

Subtract. Regroup if you need to.
Use cubes and a workmat to help.

1.

Tens	Ones
7	16
8	6
− 2	8
5	8

2.

Tens	Ones
6	8
− 2	3

3.

Tens	Ones
5	4
− 1	5

4.

Tens	Ones
7	0
− 1	6

5.

Tens	Ones
4	3
− 2	7

6.

Tens	Ones
5	7
− 1	9

7.

Tens	Ones
6	7
− 3	4

8.

Tens	Ones
3	6
− 1	7

9. Reasoning Solve. Show your work.

Jamal has 54 marbles.
Lucas has 70 marbles.
How much more marbles does
Lucas have than Jamal?

Tens	Ones
−	

Ⓐ 14

Ⓑ 16

Ⓒ 24

Ⓓ 26

Subtracting Two-Digit Numbers

Remember the steps for subtracting.

Step 1
Think: Are there enough ones to subtract?

Step 2
Regroup the ones if you need to. Subtract.

Step 3
Subtract the tens.

Write the problems in the frames. Find the difference.

38 − 13

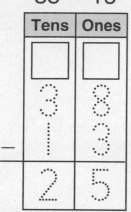

Regroup?   Yes   No

54 − 17

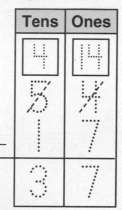

Regroup?   Yes   No

Write the problems in the frames. Find the difference.

1.   37 − 14

Tens	Ones
−	

64 − 18

Tens	Ones
−	

45 − 26

Tens	Ones
−	

73 − 25

Tens	Ones
−	

2. **Number Sense** Write a number to make this a subtraction with regrouping problem.

Tens	Ones
− 2	3

Name _____

Subtracting Two-Digit Numbers

Write the subtraction problem. Find the difference.

1. 64 − 39

Tens	Ones
5	14
6̶	4̶
− 3	9
2	5

2. 65 − 16

Tens	Ones

−

3. 72 − 31

Tens	Ones

−

4. 56 − 29

Tens	Ones

−

5. 84 − 25

Tens	Ones

−

6. 34 − 16

Tens	Ones

−

7. 96 − 48

Tens	Ones

−

8. 43 − 27

Tens	Ones

−

9. Norma has 48 buttons. Connie has 29 buttons. How many more buttons does Norma have than Connie?

Ⓐ 29 buttons

Ⓑ 21 buttons

Ⓒ 19 buttons

Ⓓ 11 buttons

10. Number Sense Use each number only once. Write and solve the subtraction problem with the greatest difference.

1 2 4 5

Tens	Ones

−

Subtracting on a Number Line

Show 19 − 13 = 6 on a number line
First, find 19 on the number line.

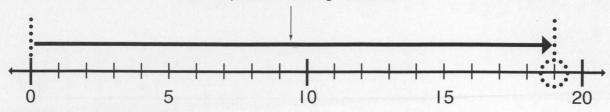

Move 19 places to the right from zero

Then, count back 13 places on the number line to
subtract 13.

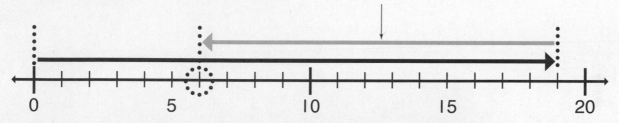

Count back 13 on the number line to subtract 13

When you count back 13, you get to 6. 6 is the
answer to the problem 19 − 13.

1. Show 16 − 12 = 4 on a number line.

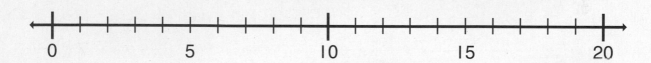

2. Journal Explain how you found 16 − 12 = 4 on
the number line.

_____

_____

_____

Subtracting on a Number Line

Show these subtraction problems on the number lines.

1. 18 − 12 = _____

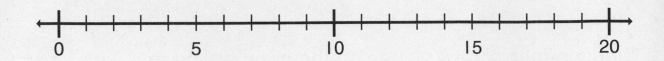

2. 14 − 10 = _____

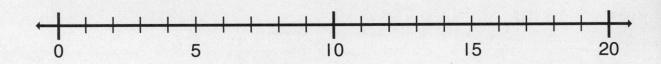

3. 15 − 11 = _____

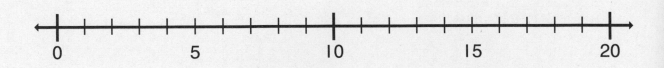

Using Addition to Check Subtraction

When you subtract,
you start with the whole.
Then you take part away.
The other part is left.

37 [Whole]
− 12 [Part]
25 [Part]

Tens	Ones

To check your work,
add to put the parts
back together.
Your answer should
be the whole.

25 [Part]
+ 12 [Part]
37 [Whole]

Tens	Ones

and   and

Subtract. Check your answer by adding.

I.

Tens	Ones
3	3
− 2	1
1	2

12
+ 21
33

2.

Tens	Ones
8	6
−	9

3.

Tens	Ones
5	4
− 1	9

4.

Tens	Ones
6	3
− 3	7

Name _____

Using Addition to Check Subtraction

Subtract. Check your answer by adding.
Write the missing part.

1.

```
  5 12
  6̶ 2̶
- 1 8
  4 4
```

```
  1
  4 4
+ 1 8
  6 2
```

2.
```
  8 3
- 2 9
```

3.
```
  7 3
- 3 7
```

4.
```
  4 8
- 2 1
```

5.
```
  9 4
- 2 8
```

6.
```
  7 5
- 1 7
```

7. Lana has 39 moon stickers and 52 star stickers. How many more star stickers than moon stickers does she have?

Ⓐ 13 more

Ⓑ 17 more

Ⓒ 23 more

Ⓓ 27 more

8. Algebra Write the number that makes each number sentence true.

60 − 20 = 20 + _____

50 − 40 = 10 + _____

70 − 30 = 10 + _____

80 − 40 = 30 + _____

Ways to Subtract

Use **mental math** to subtract $75 - 20$.
Count back 2 tens. 75, 65, 55.

$75 - 20 = \underline{55}$

Use **cubes** to subtract $38 - 12$.

Show 38. Take away 1 ten.
Then take away 2 ones.

Tens	Ones

$38 - 12 = \underline{26}$

Use **paper and pencil** to subtract $60 - 23$.

Regroup 1 ten as 10 ones.

$$\begin{array}{cc} \boxed{5} & \boxed{10} \\ \cancel{6} & \cancel{0} \\ - \ 2 & 3 \end{array}$$

$60 - 23 = \underline{37}$

Use a **calculator** to subtract $85 - 59$.

$\boxed{8}\ \boxed{5}\ \boxed{-}\ \boxed{5}\ \boxed{9}\ \boxed{=}$

$85 - 59 = \underline{26}$

Circle how you will solve the problem.
Then subtract.

1. mental math
cubes
paper and pencil
calculator

$75 - 10 = \underline{\hspace{1cm}}$

2. mental math
cubes
paper and pencil
calculator

$49 - 22 = \underline{\hspace{1cm}}$

Ways to Subtract

Circle the way you will solve the problem. Then subtract.

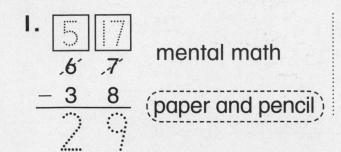

1. 5 17
    6 7
    − 3 8
    2 9

    mental math

    (paper and pencil)

2.   8 5
    − 5 4   mental math

             paper and pencil

Write the way you will solve the problem.
Then subtract and write the difference.

3. 70 − 46 = _____

    _____

4. 92 − 27 = _____

    _____

5. Melissa decorates a book cover with stickers.
   She uses 52 star stickers and 38 moon stickers.
   How many more star stickers than moon stickers did she use?

    12   14   24   26
    Ⓐ   Ⓑ   Ⓒ   Ⓓ

6. **Algebra** Fong has 80 marbles.
   He wants to give his friend 50 of them.
   Which problem shows how many marbles Fong will have left?

        8   50   80   80
      − 5   − 8   − 5   − 50
        3   42   75   30
      Ⓐ   Ⓑ   Ⓒ   Ⓓ

Problem Solving:
Two-Question Problems

Use the answer from the first question to answer the second question.

Tomas has 17 red toy cars and 8 blue toy cars. How many toy cars does he have in all?

(Follow Step 1 to answer this question.)

Tomas gives 6 cars to his brother. How many toy cars does Tomas have left?

(Use the answer from the first question in Step 1 to answer this question. Follow Step 2.)

Step 1

Add to find out how many toy cars Tomas has in all.

$$17 + 8 = 25$$

Step 2

Subtract the number of cars Tomas gives his brother.

$$25 - 6 = 19$$

Tomas has __19__ cars left.

Use the answer from the first question to answer the second question.

1. Marta picked 12 red flowers and 9 pink flowers. How many flowers did Marta pick in all?

She gives 5 flowers to her teacher. How many flowers does Marta have left?

Step 1

Add to find out how many flowers Marta picked in all.

$$\_\_\_ + \_\_\_ = \_\_\_$$

Step 2

Subtract to find out how many flowers Marta has left.

$$\_\_\_ - \_\_\_ = \_\_\_$$

Marta has _____ flowers left.

Two-Question Problems

Solve. Use the answer from the first question to answer
the second question.

1. Barb has 12 pink bows and 13 green bows.
How many bows does she have in all?   25 bows

Barb gives 9 bows to her sister.
How many bows does she have left?   16 bows

2. Amy has some eggs in a carton.
She has 16 eggs in a bowl. She has
27 eggs in all. How many eggs does
Amy have in the carton?   _____ eggs

Amanda cooks 6 of the eggs from the
carton for her family's breakfast. How
many eggs are left in the carton?   _____ eggs

3. Marcos had 20 stickers.
He used 7 stickers.
Then he used 5 stickers.

How many stickers does
Marcos have now?

Ⓐ 8

Ⓑ 12

Ⓒ 13

Ⓓ 32

4. 21 ants were on a hill.
42 ants joined them.

Later, some ants left.
Now 33 ants are on the hill.
How many ants left?

Ⓐ 21

Ⓑ 30

Ⓒ 63

Ⓓ 72

Building 1,000

Remember.

10 ones = ____ ten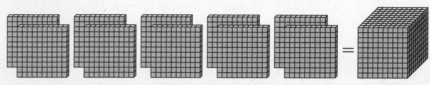

10 tens = ____ hundred

10 hundreds = ____ thousand

Count by 100s
to count hundreds.

Color the models to show the hundreds.

1. 2 hundreds
   200
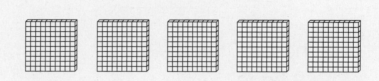

2. 3 hundreds
   300
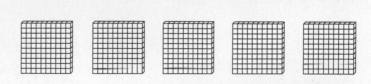

3. 4 hundreds
   400
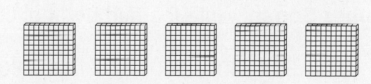

4. 5 hundreds
   500
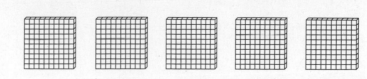

Name _____

Building 1,000

Write how many. Use models if needed.

1.

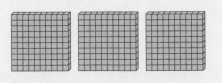

100 less is

_____.

_____

100 more is

_____.

2.

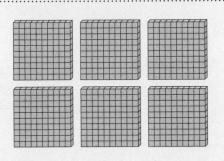

100 less is

_____.

_____

100 more is

_____.

3. Each bag has 100 pretzels.
There are 9 bags.
How many pretzels are there in all?

90	100	500	900
Ⓐ	Ⓑ	Ⓒ	Ⓓ

4. Number Sense Write the number that comes next:

100 200 300 400 500 600 700 800 900 _____

How many hundreds flats would you need to show it?

_____ hundreds flats

Counting Hundreds, Tens, and Ones

Use models and your workmat to sort and count.

First, put the hundreds models on your mat.
Next, put the tens models on your mat.
Then, put the ones models on your mat.

Write the number of hundreds, tens, and ones.

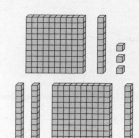

Hundreds	Tens	Ones
2	4	3

Write the numbers.
Use models and your workmat if needed.

1.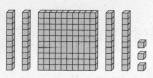

Hundreds	Tens	Ones

2.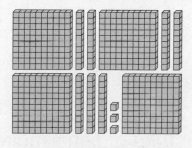

Hundreds	Tens	Ones

3. Number Sense How many hundreds are in 581? _____

Name _____

Counting Hundreds, Tens, and Ones

Write the numbers. Use models and your workmat if needed.

1.
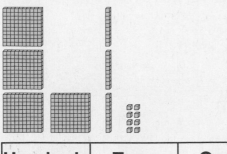

Hundreds	Tens	Ones
4	3	8

2.
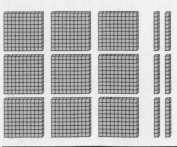

Hundreds	Tens	Ones

3.
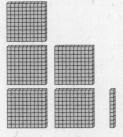

Hundreds	Tens	Ones

4.
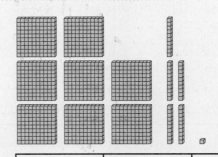

Hundreds	Tens	Ones

5. **Reasonableness** Kyra wrote **78** to match the model.

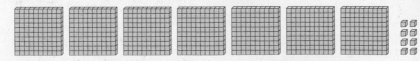

What mistake did she make?

_____

What is the correct number to match the model?

87   708   780   807

(A)   (B)   (C)   (D)

Reading and Writing Numbers to 1,000

Expanded form uses plus signs to show hundreds, tens, and ones.

200 + 60 + 4

You can draw models to show expanded form.

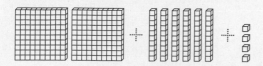

The **number word** is two hundred sixty-four.

The **standard form** is

<u>264</u>.

Draw models to show the expanded form.
Write the number in standard form.

1. 400 + 30 + 8   four hundred thirty-eight

_____

2. 300 + 70 + 2   three hundred seventy-two

_____

3. Write the number in expanded   five hundred fourteen
and standard form.

_____ + _____ + _____   _____

Reading and Writing Numbers to 1,000

Circle the models to match the expanded form.
Then write the standard form.

1. 200 + 70 + 5

two hundred
seventy-five

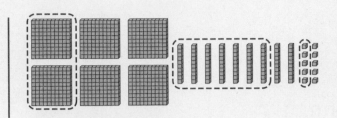

275

2. 100 + 40 + 0

one hundred
forty

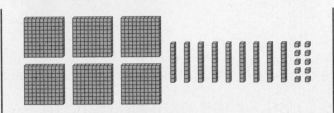

_____

3. 300 + 60 + 2

three hundred
sixty-two

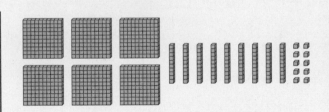

_____

4. 329 cars are parked in a parking lot.

What is the expanded form of 329?

Ⓐ 200 + 90 + 3

Ⓑ 200 + 20 + 9

Ⓒ 300 + 20 + 9

Ⓓ 300 + 90 + 2

5. Reasoning What is the greatest number you can make using these digits?

5   7   2

Ⓐ 257

Ⓑ 572

Ⓒ 725

Ⓓ 752

Changing Numbers by Hundreds and Tens

When you change a number by adding or subtracting tens, the tens digit changes.

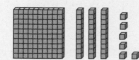

$100 + 30 + 6 = 136$

(Use mental math to think: 10 more.)

$136 + 10 = \underline{146}$

(Use mental math to think: 20 less.)

$136 - 20 = \underline{116}$

When you change a number by adding or subtracting hundreds, the hundreds digit changes.

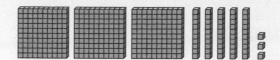

$300 + 50 + 3 = 353$

(Use mental math to think: 100 more.)

$353 + 100 = \underline{453}$

(Use mental math to think: 200 less.)

$353 - 200 = \underline{153}$

1. Use models and mental math to solve.

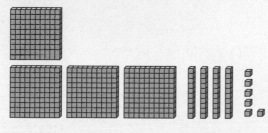

$446 + 20 = \underline{}$

$446 + 200 = \underline{}$

$400 + 40 + 6 = 446$

2. Journal Draw hundreds, tens, and ones models for 254. Show 10 more. Solve.

$254 + 10 = \underline{}$

Changing Numbers by Hundreds and Tens

Use models, drawings, or mental math to solve.
Write the numbers.

1. Start with 148.

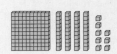

$148 + 40 = 188$

$148 + 400 = 548$

2. Start with 594.

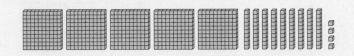

$594 - 30 = $ _____

$594 - 300 = $ _____

3. Suki has 350 points. She gets 30 more points.

How many points does Suki have now?

320	353	360	380
Ⓐ	Ⓑ	Ⓒ	Ⓓ

4. Abdul has 687 points. He loses 100 points. How many points does Abdul have now?

787	687	686	587
Ⓐ	Ⓑ	Ⓒ	Ⓓ

5. Algebra Write the number.
How many more hundreds do you need to make 500?

_____ + _____ = 500

Name _____

Patterns with Numbers on Hundreds Charts

Pick a row on the top chart. Read the numbers across the row.

11	12	13	14	15	16	17	18	19	20
21	22	23	24	25	26	27	28	29	30
31	32	33	34	35	36	37	38	39	40

The ones go up by ___ .

Pick a column and read the numbers from top to bottom.

110	111	112	113	114	115	116	117	118	119	120
210	211	212	213	214	215	216	217	218	219	220
310	311	312	313	314	315	316	317	318	319	320
410	411	412	413	414	415	416	417	418	419	420

The tens go up by ___ .

In the bottom chart, the hundreds digits from top to bottom go up by ___ .

Look at the digits. Look for a pattern.
Write the missing numbers.

I.

	33	34
42	43	
52	53	54

	77	78
86	87	
96		98

2.

43		45
53		55
		65

430		450
530		550
		650

3. Number Sense What is the rule?

60 ⟶ 70   670 ⟶ 680

Patterns with Numbers on Hundreds Charts

Write the missing numbers.

1.

52	53	54
62	63	64
72	73	74

520	530	
620		
		740

2.

		69
77	78	
		89

	680	
770		790
	880	

3.

15		
	26	
		37

	160	
250		
350		370

4. Which best describes the pattern of the numbers on the mailboxes?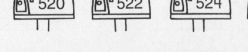

10 more	10 less	2 more	2 less
Ⓐ	Ⓑ	Ⓒ	Ⓓ

5. Number Sense Look for a pattern. What is the rule?

740   730   720   710

100 more	100 less	10 more	10 less
Ⓐ	Ⓑ	Ⓒ	Ⓓ

Skip Counting by 2, 5, 10, 100 to 1,000

You can use a number line to show skip counting.
Skip count by 5s.

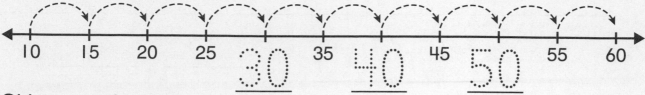

Skip count by 10s.

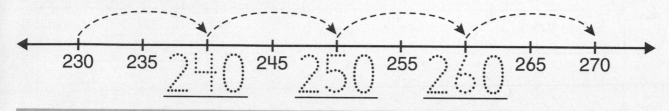

Number Sense Skip count on the number line.

1.

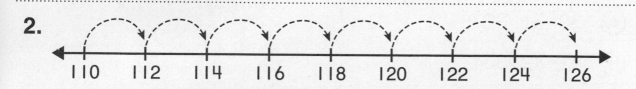

You skip counted by _____.

2.

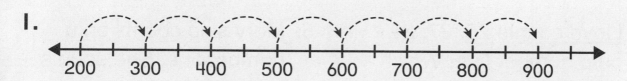

You skip counted by _____.

3. Skip count on the number line. Write the missing numbers.

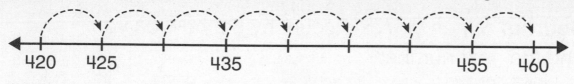

_____   _____ _____

Skip Counting by 2, 5, 10, 100 to 1,000

Skip count on the number line.
Write the missing numbers.

1.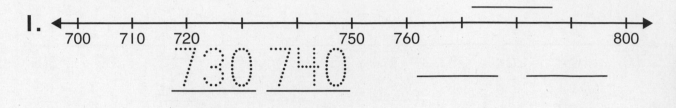

2.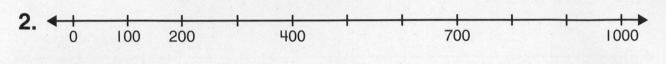

3.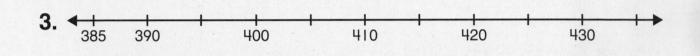

4. Lloyd counts 25, 27, 29 on a number line. Which three numbers should he count next?

(A) 30, 31, 32

(B) 31, 32, 33

(C) 31, 33, 35

(D) 32, 34, 36

5. Mary skip counts on a number line. She counts 330, 340, 350. What number does she skip count by?

(A) 2

(B) 4

(C) 5

(D) 10

6. Journal When you skip count by 5s, how do you find the next number?

_____

Name _____

Comparing Numbers

Compare the digits with the greatest place value first.

125   243

100 is <u>less than</u> 200. So, 125 (<) 243.

If the hundreds are equal, compare the tens.

243   217

40 is <u>more than</u> 10. So, 243 (>) 217.

If the tens are equal, compare the ones.

217   216

7 is <u>more than</u> 6. So, 217 (>) 216.

Compare.
Write <, >, or =.

1. 341 ◯ 432   **2.** 890 ◯ 880

3. 621 ◯ 639   **4.** 546 ◯ 546

Name _____

Comparing Numbers

Compare. Write **greater than**, **less than**, or **equal to**.
Then write >, <, or =.

1. 157 is __less than__ 214.   157 214

2. 600 is _____ 598.   600 598

3. 771 is _____ 771.   771 771

---

4. This week, 261 fans watched a soccer game.
   Last week, 216 fans watched a soccer game.
   Which comparison is correct?

   216 = 261   216 > 261   261 < 216   216 < 261
     Ⓐ   Ⓑ   Ⓒ   Ⓓ

---

5. **Spatial Thinking** Circle hundreds, tens, and
   ones to show your answer.

   This number is less than 200 and greater than 100.
   The ones digit is 5 less than 10. The tens digit is
   2 more than the ones digit. What is the number?

   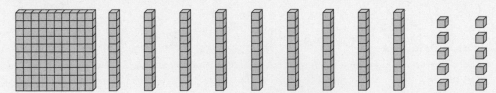

   _____

Problem Solving: Look for a Pattern

Put these numbers in order from least to greatest.

How do the numbers change each time? Look for a pattern.

240   210   230   250   220

_210_, _220_, _230_, _240_, _250_

The pattern rule is _+10_.

Look for a number pattern to solve.

1.

Put the room number signs in order from least to greatest.

_300_, _305_,

_____, _____

The pattern rule is _____.

What room number would

come next? _____

2.

Put the taxis in order by number from least to greatest.

_____, _____,

_____, _____

The pattern rule is _____.

What taxi number would

come next? _____

Problem Solving: Look for a Pattern

Look for a number pattern to solve.

1.

Put the numbers on the bears in order from least to greatest.

616, 636, 656, ____

What is the pattern rule?

+20

What is the next number?

696

2.

Put the numbers on the geese in order from least to greatest.

_____, _____,

_____, _____

What is the pattern rule?

_____

What is the next number?

_____

---

3. What is the next mailbox number?

751	791	841	881
Ⓐ	Ⓑ	Ⓒ	Ⓓ

---

4. Algebra Look at the pattern. What is the missing number?
423, 425, ____, 429

421	426	427	435
Ⓐ	Ⓑ	Ⓒ	Ⓓ

Name _____

Exploring Adding Three-Digit Numbers

There are different ways to add.
Find 358 + 213.

Add hundreds.	Add tens.	Add ones.	Add the sums.
300	50	8	500
+ 200	+ 10	+ 3	60
500	60	11	+ 11
			571

So, 358 + 213 = _571_ .

- -

Use easier numbers.   213 = _200_ + _10_ + _3_

Add 200 to 358.	Then add 10.	Then add 3.
358	558	568
+ 200	+ 10	+ 3
558	568	571

So, 358 + 213 = _571_ .

Add any way you choose.
Use models if needed.

1. 155 + 307

155 + 307 = 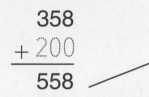 462

2. 248 + 455

248 + 455 = _____

- -

3. 209 + 376

209 + 376 = _____

4. 597 + 122

597 + 122 = _____

Exploring Adding Three-Digit Numbers

Add any way you choose.
Use models if needed. Show your work.

1. $224 + 103$

2. $417 + 215$

$224 + 103 =$ _____

$417 + 215 =$ _____

3. $351 + 398$

4. $196 + 576$

$351 + 398 =$ _____

$196 + 576 =$ _____

Algebra Find the missing number.

5. ___ $- 507 = 285$

782	785	792	802
Ⓐ	Ⓑ	Ⓒ	Ⓓ

6. ___ $+ 310 = 820$

410	510	520	610
Ⓐ	Ⓑ	Ⓒ	Ⓓ

Mental Math

Use mental math to add these three-digit numbers: 315 + 200.
You just need to add the hundreds.
Only the hundreds digit will change.

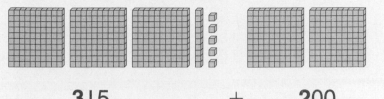

315   +   **2**00   = ___5___ 15

Add using mental math. Complete the addition sentence.

1. 323 + 200

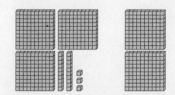

323 + 200 = 523

2. 281 + 400

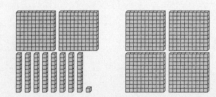

_____ + 400 = _____

3. 193 + 500

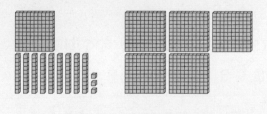

_____ + 500 = _____

4. 487 + 300

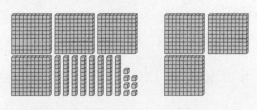

_____ + 300 = _____

5. Add using mental math. Use models if needed.

560 + 300 = _____

Name _____

Mental Math

Add using mental math. Use models if needed.

1. 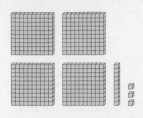 and 300

_____ + _____ = _____

2. 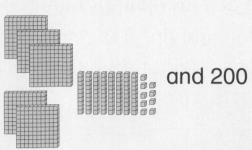 and 200

_____ + _____ = _____

3. 718 + 200 = _____

4. 605 + 300 = _____

5. 400 + 234 = _____

6. 600 + 241 = _____

7. Tanner has 500 star stickers. She has 179 rainbow stickers. How many stickers does Tanner have in all?

479   500   579   679
Ⓐ   Ⓑ   Ⓒ   Ⓓ

8. Darrin has 274 basketball stickers. He has 300 football stickers. How many stickers does Darrin have in all?

163   279   574   682
Ⓐ   Ⓑ   Ⓒ   Ⓓ

9. Algebra Write the missing numbers that make these number sentences true.

400 + 500 = 600 + _____   _____ = 899 + 100

Name _____

Estimating Sums

You can estimate the sum of 135 + 337.
Is it greater than or less than 500?

One way to estimate:
Step 1: Add 300 to 135.

135 + 300 = 435.

Step 2: Look at the tens and ones in **337**.

So, 435 + **37** is less than 500.

Another way to estimate:
Step 1: Add the hundreds in both numbers.

135 + 337 = 400.

Step 2: Look at the tens in both numbers.
30 + 30 = 60
So, 400 + 60 is less than 500.

Follow the steps to estimate.

Is 179 + 267 greater than or less than 600?

1. Add 200 to 179. 179 + 200 = _____

2. Look at the tens and ones in **267.** Then circle greater than or less than.

greater than
379 + 67 is   600.
less than

Choose a way to estimate. Circle greater than or less than.

3.   greater than
237 + 417 is   600.
less than

Name _____

Estimating Sums

Do the two buckets have more cherries or fewer cherries than the tub can hold? Circle more or fewer.

1.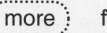

(more)　fewer

2.

more　fewer

3.

more　fewer

4. There are 314 apples in baskets. There are 281 apples still on the trees. Are there 600 apples in all? Explain.

_____

5. One week, a group of chimpanzees ate 437 bananas. The next week, they ate 465 bananas. Did they eat more than 900 bananas during both weeks? Explain.

_____

6. Estimation Which problem has a sum that is less than 400?

329 + 161　　216 + 251　　245 + 198　　262 + 126

Models for Adding with Three-Digit Numbers

135 + 248 = _____

Step 1: Add the ones. Regroup if you need to.
Step 2: Add the tens. Regroup if you need to.
Step 3: Add the hundreds.

Hundreds	Tens	Ones
135		
248		

> 5 + 8 = 13 ones. Regroup 10 ones for 1 ten.

135 + 248 = **383**

Add. Regroup if needed.
Use models and your workmat.

1.

Hundreds	Tens	Ones

341 + 127 = **468**

2.

Hundreds	Tens	Ones

524 + 249 = _____

Name _____

Models for Adding with Three-Digit Numbers

Add. Regroup if needed. Use models and your workmat to help you.

1.

Hundreds	Tens	Ones
☐	☐	
6	3	4
+ 2	1	8

2.

Hundreds	Tens	Ones
☐	☐	
5	9	3
+ 1	3	9

3.

Hundreds	Tens	Ones
☐	☐	
7	6	5
+ 1	8	0

4.

Hundreds	Tens	Ones
☐	☐	
3	5	6
+ 4	3	4

5.

Hundreds	Tens	Ones
☐	☐	
2	7	6
+ 5	9	3

6.

Hundreds	Tens	Ones
☐	☐	
4	4	1
+ 1	9	9

7. A fire truck traveled 267 miles in July to put out fires. It traveled 398 miles in August to put out fires. Which problem shows the total number of miles for both months?

Ⓐ
```
  1 1
  2 6 7
+ 3 9 8
  6 6 5
```

Ⓑ
```
  1 1
  2 7 6
+ 3 9 8
  6 7 4
```

Ⓒ
```
  1
  2 6 7
+ 3 9 8
  6 5 5
```

Ⓓ
```
  1
  2 6 7
+ 3 9 8
  5 6 5
```

8. Reasonableness George thinks that 515 plus 381 is 896. Markita says that George forgot to regroup.
Do you have to regroup to add 515 and 381? Explain.

_____

_____

Adding Three-Digit Numbers

Step 1: Add the ones. Regroup if you need to.
Step 2: Add the tens. Regroup if you need to.
Step 3: Add the hundreds.

Think:
Regroup 10 tens
for 1 hundred.

$163 + 174 =$ ___?___

Hundreds	Tens	Ones

Hundreds	Tens	Ones
1	6	3
+ 1	7	4
3	3	7

Draw to regroup. Add.

1. $218 + 136 =$ ___?___

Hundreds	Tens	Ones

Hundreds	Tens	Ones
2	1	8
+ 1	3	6
		4

Add. Use models and your workmat.

2.

Hundreds	Tens	Ones
1	2	5
+ 2	4	2

3.

Hundreds	Tens	Ones
4	1	9
+ 2	5	6

Adding Three-Digit Numbers

Add. Use models if needed.

1.	2.	3.	4.
4 7 2 + 3 4 7	6 0 9 + 1 6 6	2 6 7 + 2 2 8	4 7 3 + 3 3 8

5.	6.	7.	8.
3 1 4 + 5 9 9	1 8 6 + 3 5 7	4 8 7 + 5 1 2	2 2 5 + 1 3 5

9.	10.	11.	12.
2 3 5 + 1 4 6	4 6 5 + 2 6 4	3 0 8 + 2 3 8	3 5 6 + 1 2 9

13. One summer, an airplane made 326 trips.
The next summer, the airplane made 392 trips.
How many trips did the airplane make during both summers?

192   618   718   798
Ⓐ   Ⓑ   Ⓒ   Ⓓ

14. **Reasoning** Caitlin's paper shows
how she added 345 and 271.
What mistake did she make?

```
   3 4 5
 + 2 7 1
   5 1 6
```

_____

_____

Name _____

Exploring Subtracting Three-Digit Numbers

There are many ways to subtract.
Find 361 − 142.

One way is to count back.

Start at 361 and count back 142.

> Remember, 142 is
> 1 hundred, 4 tens, and 2 ones.

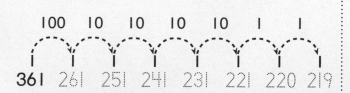

So, 361 − 142 = __219__.

Another way is to use easier numbers.

> 140 is easier to subtract than
> 142. 142 = 140 + 2

Subtract 140.
Then subtract 2 more.

```
  361            221
− 140          −  2
  221          219
```

So, 361 − 142 = __219__.

Subtract any way you choose.
Use models if needed.

1. 576 − 249

576 − 249 = __327__

2. 412 − 166

412 − 166 = ____

3. 398 − 235

398 − 235 = ____

4. 753 − 308

753 − 308 = ____

R 11·6

Name _____

Exploring Subtracting Three-Digit Numbers

Subtract any way you choose.
Use models if needed. Show your work.

1. 953 − 602

953 − 602 = _____

2. 872 − 425

872 − 425 = _____

3. 517 − 291

517 − 291 = _____

4. 634 − 386

634 − 386 = _____

5. Algebra Which is the missing number?

265 − _____ = 138

Ⓐ 27

Ⓑ 73

Ⓒ 127

Ⓓ 403

6. Mariko had 521 stamps. She gave away 118 stamps. How many stamps does she have now?

_____ stamps

Mental Math: Ways to Find Missing Parts

Count on by hundreds and tens to find the parts of the whole.

260 + _____ = 700

First, count on by hundreds. ___4___ hundreds

260, _360_, _460_, _560_, _660_
        100   200   300   400

Next, count on by tens. ___4___ tens

660, _670_, _680_, _690_, _700_
        10   20   30   40

4 hundreds and 4 tens is 440.

So, 260 + _440_ = 700.

700

| 260 | 440 |

---

1. 350 + __?__ = 600

Count on by hundreds. ___2___ hundreds

350, _450_, _550_

Count on by tens. _____ tens

550, _____, _____, _____, _____, _____

_____ hundreds and _____ tens is _____.

So, 350 + _____ = 600.

Name _____

Mental Math: Ways to Find Missing Parts

Count on or count back to find the missing part. Write the number.

1. 420 + _____ = 960

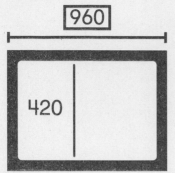

2. _____ + 190 = 630

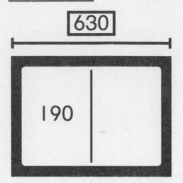

3. Clyde and Javier counted a total of 450 sheep.
Javier counted 225 sheep.
How many sheep did Clyde count?

225   250   325   450
Ⓐ   Ⓑ   Ⓒ   Ⓓ

4. Geometry Which weight is needed to balance the scale?

Ⓐ

Ⓑ

Ⓒ

Ⓓ

Estimating Differences

Estimate the difference: 596 − 221.

First, find the nearest hundred.
Is 596 closer to 500 or 600?   600

Is 221 closer to 200 or 300?   200

Then, subtract.

600 − 200 = 400

So, 596 − 221 is about 400.

Estimate each difference. First find the nearest hundred.
Then circle the estimate that matches the problem.

1. 502 − 105 is about   200   300   (400)

500 − 100 = ?

2. 609 − 403 is about   200   300   400

_____ − _____ = ?

3. 511 − 298 is about   100   200   300

_____ − _____ = ?

4. Number Sense 881 − 500 is about _____.

Estimating Differences

Circle the problem that matches the estimate.

1. about 200   820 − 205   or   (421 − 196)

2. about 400   637 − 231   or   794 − 512

3. about 300   679 − 199   or   916 − 593

4. about 600   909 − 287   or   726 − 204

5. Marcus has to put about 100 cans on a shelf to finish his job. Which box of cans should he put on the shelf?

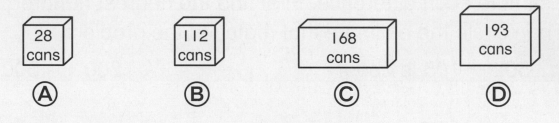

28 cans	112 cans	168 cans	193 cans
Ⓐ	Ⓑ	Ⓒ	Ⓓ

6. Estimation Cowhand Dusty put 203 cows inside of the fences. There are 694 cows in the herd. About how many more cows does Dusty need to put inside of the fences?

   Ⓐ   about 300 cows

   Ⓑ   about 400 cows

   Ⓒ   about 500 cows

   Ⓓ   about 600 cows

Models for Subtracting with Three-Digit Numbers

327 − 164 = _____

Step 1: Subtract the ones. Regroup if you need to.

Step 2: Subtract the tens. Regroup if you need to.

Step 3: Subtract the hundreds.

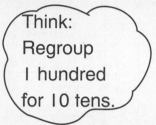

Think:
Regroup
1 hundred
for 10 tens.

Hundreds	Tens	Ones

327 − 164 = 163

Subtract to find the difference.
Use models and your workmat.

1.

Hundreds	Tens	Ones

549 − 295 = _____

2.

Hundreds	Tens	Ones

835 − 516 = _____

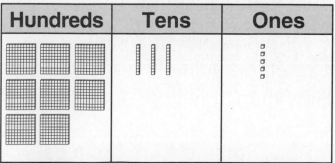

Models for Subtracting with Three-Digit Numbers

Use models and your workmat. Subtract. Regroup if needed.

1.

Hundreds	Tens	Ones
☐	☐	☐
7	5	5
− 2	8	2

2.

Hundreds	Tens	Ones
☐	☐	☐
4	8	5
− 1	3	9

3.

Hundreds	Tens	Ones
☐	☐	☐
5	7	8
− 2	9	7

4.

Hundreds	Tens	Ones
☐	☐	☐
6	5	7
− 1	2	8

5.

Hundreds	Tens	Ones
☐	☐	☐
7	3	2
− 4	5	8

6.

Hundreds	Tens	Ones
☐	☐	☐
9	2	7
− 3	0	4

7. One building is 332 feet tall. Another building is 208 feet tall. How much taller is the first building?

540 feet ⒜   136 feet ⒝   134 feet ⒞   124 feet ⒟

8. Spatial Thinking Use the model to help you subtract.

A farm has 319 animals.
136 of the animals are pigs.
How many animals are not pigs?

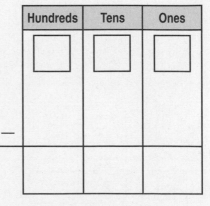

_____ animals are not pigs.

Subtracting Three-Digit Numbers

Step 1: Subtract the ones. Regroup if you need to.
Step 2: Subtract the tens. Regroup if you need to.
Step 3: Subtract the hundreds.

Think: Regroup 1 ten for 10 ones.

$362 - 125 =$ _____

Hundreds	Tens	Ones

Hundreds	Tens	Ones
	5	12
3	6	2
− 1	2	5
2	3	7

Draw to regroup. Subtract.

1. $429 - 174 =$ ___?___

Hundreds	Tens	Ones

Hundreds	Tens	Ones
4	2	9
− 1	7	4

Subtract. Use models and your workmat if needed.

2.

Hundreds	Tens	Ones
5	7	4
− 2	1	3

3.

Hundreds	Tens	Ones
7	8	8
− 2	6	9

Name _____

Subtracting Three-Digit Numbers

Subtract. Use models if needed.

1. 4 2 6
    − 2 7 1

2. 6 5 9
    − 3 7 2

3. 9 5 3
    − 2 0 9

4. 3 9 0
    − 1 2 6

5. 5 6 2
    − 1 2 9

6. 4 8 6
    − 3 5 7

7. 9 1 7
    − 5 8 2

8. 6 2 5
    − 1 3 5

9. 5 8 9
    − 1 9 3

10. 7 0 7
    − 2 6 4

11. 6 4 3
    − 2 2 8

12. 3 5 6
    − 1 2 9

13. There were 926 wild horses in a valley. Then 456 horses ran away. How many horses are left in the valley?

530   582   470   469

Ⓐ   Ⓑ   Ⓒ   Ⓓ

14. **Number Sense** Use these numbers below only once to finish the two subtraction problems. Then subtract.

2   5   7   1   4   6

Make the greatest difference.   Make the least difference.

    9 5 0   9 5 0
  − ☐ ☐ ☐   − ☐ ☐ ☐

Problem Solving: Use Logical Reasoning

Kate counted the books in her classroom library.
Clue 1: The number of books is an even number.
Clue 2: The number of books is between 200 and 300.
Clue 3: The number of books is the sum of two of the numbers below.

180   162   115   194   126

What are the two numbers?

Start with Clue 1. You can add two even numbers
or two odd numbers to get an even sum. 115 is the
only odd number. Cross out 115.

Then use Clue 2. 180 + 126, 162 + 126, and
194 + 126 are close to 300.

Add to find their sums.
180 + 126 = 306   162 + 126 = 288   194 + 126 = 320
288 is between 200 and 300.

The two numbers are __162__ and __126__.

Use the clues to solve the riddle.

1. When Steve rides in the car, he counts trucks.
   He counts an odd number of trucks.
   The number of trucks is between 300 and 400.
   The number of trucks is the sum of two of the numbers below.

   234   175   180   291   116

   What are the two numbers?

   _____ and _____

Problem Solving: Use Logical Reasoning

Use the clues to solve the riddles.

1. Diego made a castle with small building blocks.
He used an even number of blocks.
The number of blocks is between 700 and 800.
The number of blocks is the sum of two of the numbers below.

352   476   326   423   284

What are the two numbers? _____ and _____

2. Abby counts the oranges she picks.
She counted between 400 and 500 oranges.
The number of oranges is an odd number.
The number of oranges is the sum of two of the numbers below.

137   258   114   164   281

What are the two numbers? _____ and _____

3. Max saves quarters.
The number of quarters he has saved is
between 300 and 400. It is an even number.
The number of quarters is the sum of two of the numbers below.

215   248   137   226   182

What are the two numbers?

137 and 248   182 and 226   215 and 137   248 and 182
     Ⓐ   Ⓑ   Ⓒ   Ⓓ

Flat Surfaces, Vertices, and Edges

Some solid figures have **flat surfaces** or **faces**. Some have **edges** and **vertices**.

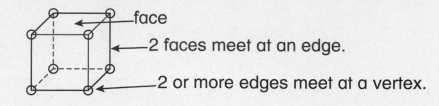

face
2 faces meet at an edge.
2 or more edges meet at a vertex.

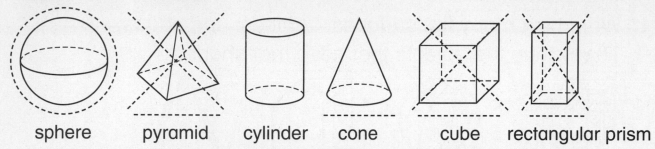

sphere   pyramid   cylinder   cone   cube   rectangular prism

Put an X on the solid figures that have edges.
Underline the solid figures that have vertices.
Circle the solid figure that does not have a flat surface.

Write the number of flat surfaces or faces, edges, and vertices. Use solid figures to help you.

1.

flat surfaces __2__

edges _____

vertices _____

2.

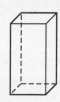

faces _____

edges _____

vertices _____

Flat Surfaces, Vertices, and Edges

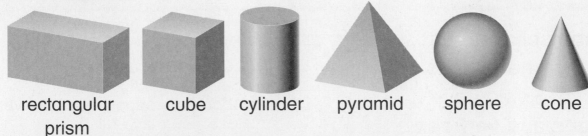

rectangular   cube   cylinder   pyramid   sphere   cone
prism

1. Write how many flat surfaces, vertices, and edges.
Then circle the objects that have that shape.

A rectangular prism has __6__ faces, ___ vertices, and ___ edges.

2. Ming's shape has 2 flat surfaces. It has no edges and no vertices. What shape is it?

Ⓐ
Ⓑ
Ⓒ
Ⓓ

3. Kim's shape has no flat surfaces. It has no edges and no vertices. What shape is it?

Ⓐ
Ⓑ
Ⓒ
Ⓓ

4. Algebra How many edges do these two shapes have in all? Write a number sentence.

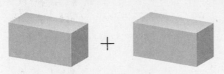

____ + ____ = ____

The two shapes have ____ edges in all.

Relating Plane Shapes to Solid Figures

If you trace the flat surfaces, or faces of solid figures, you will get these plane shapes.

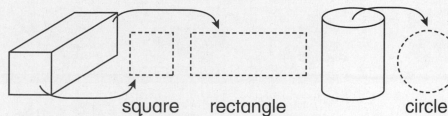

square   rectangle   circle   triangle

Use solid figures in your classroom.
Trace one flat surface or face.
Write the name of the shape you traced.

1.

_____

2.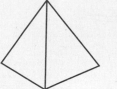

_____

3.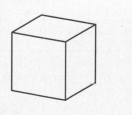

_____

4.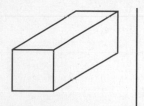

_____

Relating Plane Shapes to Solid Figures

Circle the solid figure or figures that have flat surfaces or faces you can trace to make the plane shape.

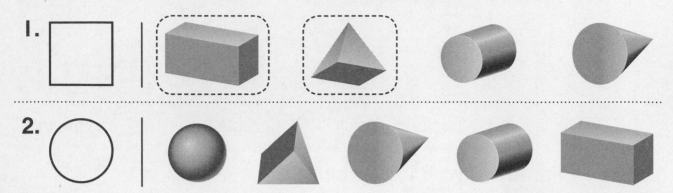

3. Dionne traces a square using a solid shape. Which solid shape does he have?

Ⓐ
Ⓑ
Ⓒ
Ⓓ

4. Which object did Maggie use to trace the rectangle?

Ⓐ 
Ⓑ
Ⓒ GUM
Ⓓ

5. Geometry Circle the block or blocks Vincent can trace to draw the bug.

Name _____

Polygons and Angles

 A triangle has
3 sides,
3 angles, and
3 vertices.

 A quadrilateral has
4 sides,
4 angles, and
4 vertices.

 A pentagon has
5 sides,
5 angles, and
5 vertices.

 A hexagon has
6 sides,
6 angles, and
6 vertices.

Match the shapes with the words.

1. Pentagon   **2.** Quadrilateral   **3.** Hexagon   **4.** Triangle

   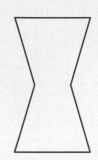   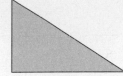   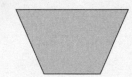

5. Describe how you were able to tell the shapes apart.

_____

_____

Name _____

Polygons and Angles

Name the shape shown below. Tell about
the attributes of the shapes.

I.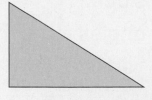

_____ sides

_____ vertices

_____ angles

Shape: _____

2.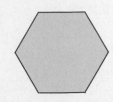

_____ sides

_____ vertices

_____ angles

Shape: _____

Draw the shape and tell how many sides, angles, and vertices.

3. Pentagon

_____ sides

_____ vertices

_____ angles

4. Quadrilateral

_____ sides

_____ vertices

_____ angles

Wholes and Equal Parts

Equal parts are the same shape and size.

 equal parts

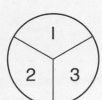

(halves)

thirds

fourths

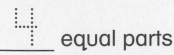 equal parts

halves

(thirds)

fourths

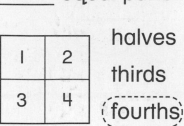 equal parts

halves

thirds

(fourths)

How many equal parts? Write the number of parts.
Circle halves, thirds, or fourths.

1. _____ equal parts

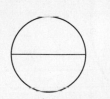

halves

thirds

fourths

2. _____ equal parts

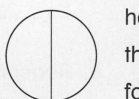

halves

thirds

fourths

3. _____ equal parts

halves

thirds

fourths

4. _____ equal parts

halves

thirds

fourths

5. _____ equal parts

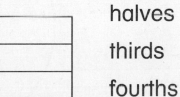

halves

thirds

fourths

6. _____ equal parts

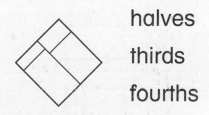

halves

thirds

fourths

7. Spatial Thinking Draw lines to show 2 equal parts.

Wholes and Equal Parts

Write the number of parts.
Circle **equal** or **unequal**.

1.

 (equal) unequal parts

2.

_____ equal unequal parts

Draw a line or lines to show equal parts.

3. fourths

4. thirds

5. Sami has a paper rectangle. Which shows how she could cut it into halves?

Ⓐ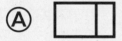

Ⓑ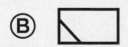

Ⓒ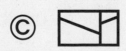

Ⓓ

6. Reasoning Circle **yes** or **no**. Can the heart be divided into 2 equal parts?

yes   no

Dividing Rectangles into Equal Squares

How many squares cover this rectangle?

Count the squares by rows:

$3 + 3 = 6$

Count the squares by columns:

$2 + 2 + 2 = 6$

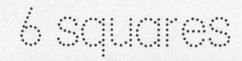

---

1. How many squares cover the rectangle?

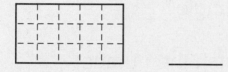 _____

2. Write number sentences to tell how you counted...

by rows:

_____

by columns:

_____

Dividing Rectangles into Equal Squares

Use square tiles to cover the rectangle.

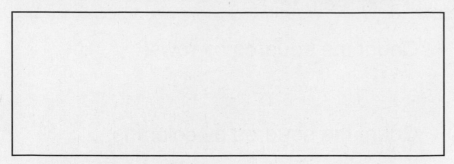

1. Write number sentences to tell how you counted by rows and columns.

Count by rows: _____

Count by columns: _____

2. How many squares covered the rectangle? _____

3. Which of the following rectangles match the number sentences?

Count by rows: 3 + 3 + 3 = 9

Count by columns: 3 + 3 + 3 = 9

  Ⓐ   Ⓑ   Ⓒ   Ⓓ

4. Reasoning Circle *Yes* or *No*. A rectangle can be made using only one row of square tiles.

Yes   No

Equal Shares, Different Shapes

You can divide a rectangle into equal shares.

The equal shares can be different shapes.

For shares to be equal, they must be the same size.

This rectangle shows 2 equal shares.

How many squares are in

each equal share? __3__

Draw lines to divide the rectangles into equal shares.
Write the number of squares in each equal share.

1.

How many squares in each equal share? _____

2.

How many squares in each equal share? _____

Equal Shares, Different Shapes

1. Draw lines to show two different ways to divide the rectangle into 3 equal shares.

2. How do you know the shares are equal?

_____

_____

3. How many squares are in each equal share? _____

4. Reasoning Which rectangle does **NOT** show 2 equal shares?

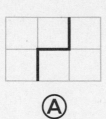
Ⓐ

Ⓑ

Ⓒ

Ⓓ

Name _____

Problem Solving:
Use Reasoning

Read the clues.

I am not a square.
I do not have 4 sides.
Which shape am I?

To find the shape, think:
It is not a square, so cross out the square.

It does not have 4 sides, so cross out the shape with 4 sides.

Circle the shape that fits the clues.

Cross out the solid figures or shapes that do not fit the clues. Circle the shape or solid figure that answers the question.

1. I do not have edges.
I am not a pyramid.
Which shape am I?

....

2. I do not have 6 sides.
I am not a circle.
Which shape am I?

Name _____

Problem Solving: Use Reasoning

Cross out shapes that do not match the clues.
Circle the shape that answers the question.

1. Which shape am I?
I have 3 sides and 3 vertices.
The lengths of my sides are equal.

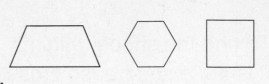

2. Which shape am I?
I have more than 5 sides.
The lengths of my sides are equal.

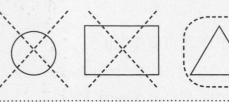

3. Which shape am I?
I have 5 flat surfaces. You can
trace my flat surfaces to make
a triangle and a rectangle.

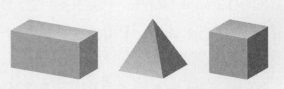

4. I have no vertices or edges.
I have 2 flat surfaces.
Which shows my shape?

Ⓐ

Ⓑ

Ⓒ

Ⓓ

5. Reasonableness I have
4 sides. The lengths of my
sides are not equal. Which
shows my shape?

Ⓐ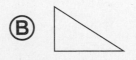

Ⓑ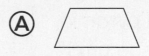

Ⓒ

Ⓓ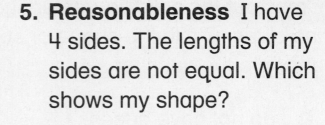

Coins

 quarter
25 cents
25¢

 half-dollar
50 cents
50¢

Start with 25¢. Count on by fives. | Start with 50¢. Count on by tens.

Think: 25¢   5¢ more   5¢ more | Think: 50¢   10¢ more   10¢ more

         |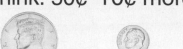

25¢   30¢   35¢   50¢   60¢   70¢

Count on to find the total amount.
Use coins if you need to.

1. Start with 25¢. Count on by tens.

Total Amount

25¢ ____ ____ ____ ____

2. Start with 50¢. Count on by tens and ones.

Total Amount

____ ____ ____ ____ ____

3. Number Sense Draw coins so the
hand holds 40¢.

Name _____

Coins

Count on to find the total amount.

1.

Total Amount
70¢

25¢ 50¢ 60¢ ____ ____

2.

Total Amount

____ ____ ____ ____ ____

3. Which group of coins has a value of 90¢?

Ⓐ

Ⓑ

Ⓒ

Ⓓ

4. Reasoning Jamal has these coins:

He needs 85¢ to buy a toy car.
Draw another coin so that Jamal has
enough money to buy the toy car.

Counting Collections of Coins

To count coins, start with the coin that has the greatest value. Count on coins from the greatest to the least value.

Find the total amount.
Draw an X on the coin with the greatest value.

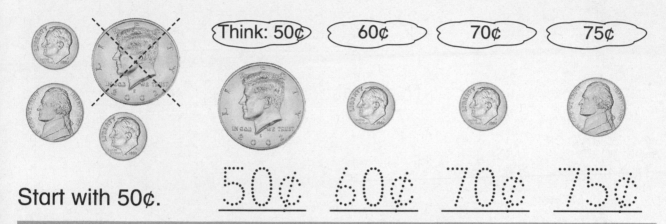

Think: 50¢   60¢   70¢   75¢

Start with 50¢.   50¢ 60¢ 70¢ 75¢

Draw an X on the coin with the greatest value.
Count on to find the total amount.

1.

Start with _____. _____ _____ _____ _____

2.

Start with _____. _____ _____ _____ _____

Name _____

Counting Collections of Coins

Draw the coins from the greatest to the least value.
Count on to find the total amount. You can use coins.

1.

 ⌜10¢⌝

25¢ 35¢ _____ _____

The total amount is __46¢__.

2.

_____ _____ _____ _____

The total amount is _____.

---

3. Karen has 85 cents.
She has a half dollar and
a dime. Which other coin
does Karen have?

Ⓐ

Ⓑ

Ⓒ

Ⓓ

4. **Estimation** Kobe has about
50¢. Circle the coins he
might have.

Name _____

Ways to Show the Same Amount

A **dollar bill** is equal to 100¢. Remember to use a **dollar sign** and **decimal point** when you write $1.00.

100 pennies = **1 dollar**

$$100¢ = \$1.00$$

Circle coins to show $1.00.
Write the number of coins.

1.

_____ dimes = 1 dollar

2.

_____ quarters = 1 dollar

3.

_____ half-dollars = 1 dollar

4. Algebra What 2 coins will make the statement true?

     = $1.00

Name _____

Ways to Show the Same Amount

Write each total amount.
Circle sets of coins that equal $1.00.

1.

Total Amount
$1.00

2.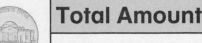

Total Amount

---

3. Ed has these coins.

How much money does
he need to make a dollar?

Ⓐ 1¢

Ⓑ 5¢

Ⓒ 10¢

Ⓓ 25¢

4. Number Sense Pam has
4 coins. The coins total
100¢. Circle the coins
that Pam has.

One Dollar

How much money?
Start counting with the dollar bill.
Then count the coins from the greatest to least value.
Write numbers to show the counting order.

_3_   _2_   _1_   _4_

Count on to find the total amount.

$1.36
Total
Amount

          +25   +10   +1

$1.00 $1.25 $1.35 $1.36

How much money? Count on to find the total amount.

1.

Total
Amount

$1.00 $2.00 _____ _____   _____

2.

Total
Amount

_____ _____ _____ _____   _____

One Dollar

Count on to find the total amount.

1.

Total
Amount

$2 $3 $3.50 | $3.50

2.

Total
Amount

_____ _____ _____ | _____

3.

Total
Amount

_____ _____ _____ | _____

---

4. Algebra Abby needs 5 dollars to go to the movie. She has the money shown at the right in her purse. How much money does she need to make 5 dollars?

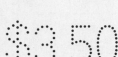   

Ⓐ   Ⓑ   Ⓒ   Ⓓ

Problem Solving:
Make an Organized List

How many ways can you make 25¢?
Two ways are shown in the chart.

Use coins to help you find another way.
Show 1 dime. Make 1 tally mark.

How many nickels do you need to make 15¢?

3
___

Make 3 tally marks.

Ways to Show 25¢			
Quarter	Dime	Nickel	Total Amount
I			25¢
	I I	I	25¢
	I	I I I	25¢

Show 3 ways to make 45¢.
Use tally marks (/) to record the coins.

Ways to Show 45¢			
Quarter	Dime	Nickel	Total Amount
			45¢
			45¢
			45¢

Problem Solving:
Make an Organized List

Use coins. Finish the list.

1. Adrian wants to buy a plum for 80¢. He has half dollars, quarters, and dimes. Find all the ways he can make 80¢.

Half Dollar	Quarter	Dime	Total Amount
⋮		⦙⦙⦙	80¢
			80¢
			80¢

2. Beth wants to buy some crackers for 23¢. She has dimes, nickels, and pennies. Find all the ways she can make 23¢.

Dime	Nickel	Penny	Total Amount
II		III	23¢
			23¢
	IIII		23¢
			23¢

3. How many ways can Adrian make 80¢?

Ⓐ 1 way

Ⓑ 2 ways

Ⓒ 3 ways

Ⓓ 4 ways

4. Which coins would Beth use to pay for the crackers with the fewest number of coins?

Ⓐ dimes and nickels

Ⓑ nickels and pennies

Ⓒ pennies

Ⓓ dimes and pennies

5. **Reasonableness** Circle **yes** or **no**.
Can you make 38¢ with these coins?

     yes   no

Adding Money

Adding money is the same as adding two-digit numbers.

Add two-digit numbers

Tens	Ones
⁝	
3	5
+ 2	8
6	3

Add money.

Tens	Ones
⁝	
3	5¢
+ 2	8¢
6	3¢

Remember to write
the ¢ sign in your answer.

Add to find the total amount.

1.

Tens	Ones
1	8
+ 4	7
6	5

Tens	Ones
1	8¢
+ 4	7¢

2.

Tens	Ones
3	3
+ 2	5

Tens	Ones
3	3¢
+ 2	5¢

3. Estimation Sarah spends 25¢ on an apple.
Sarah has 60¢. Does she have enough ¢ to
buy juice for 39¢ too? Circle **yes** or **no**.

yes   no

25¢

39¢

Name _____

Adding Money

Add to find the total amount.

1.
```
    2 | 4 ¢
  + 4 | 8 ¢
  ---------
    7 | 2 ¢
```

2.
```
    5 | 5 ¢
  + 3 | 6 ¢
  ---------
```

3.
```
    2 | 9 ¢
  + 2 | 6 ¢
  ---------
```

4.
```
    1 | 8 ¢
  + 6 | 4 ¢
  ---------
```

5.
```
    2 | 4 ¢
  + 4 | 3 ¢
  ---------
```

6.
```
    3 | 8 ¢
  + 4 | 7 ¢
  ---------
```

7.
```
    5 | 9 ¢
  + 2 | 0 ¢
  ---------
```

8.
```
    2 | 6 ¢
  + 6 | 7 ¢
  ---------
```

9. Carlos buys a toy car for 38¢.
Jessica buys a toy car for 46¢.
How much money did they spend in all?

84¢   82¢   76¢   72¢
Ⓐ   Ⓑ   Ⓒ   Ⓓ

10. Della buys a taco for 62¢.
She buys taco sauce for 18¢.
How much money did Della spend in all?

70¢   76¢   80¢   84¢
Ⓐ   Ⓑ   Ⓒ   Ⓓ

11. Reasonableness Wade added 61¢ and 28¢.
His answer was 89¢. Was he correct? Explain.

_____

Subtracting Money

Subtracting money is the same as subtracting two-digit numbers.

```
  5 1¢
- 2 2¢
```

Think of the pennies as ones and the dimes as tens.

Tens	Ones
4	11
5̷	1̷¢
− 2	2¢
2	9¢

Remember to write the cents sign in your answer.

Subtract to find the difference.

1.

```
□ □        □ □        □ □        □ □
5  9¢      6  5¢      7  3¢      4  2¢
-2  4¢     -2  4¢     -5  7¢     -2  8¢
3  5¢
```

2.

```
□ □        □ □        □ □        □ □
8  0¢      7  2¢      6  0¢      4  8¢
-2  9¢     -3  6¢     -4  8¢     -1  8¢
```

3. Reasoning Greg has 58¢. He spends 25¢. How much money does Greg have left?

□ □

Greg has _____ left.

Subtracting Money

Subtract to find the difference.

1.
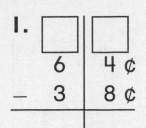

$$
\begin{array}{r}
6\ \ 4¢ \\
-\ 3\ \ 8¢ \\
\hline
\end{array}
$$

2.

$$
\begin{array}{r}
8\ \ 3¢ \\
-\ 3\ \ 9¢ \\
\hline
\end{array}
$$

3.
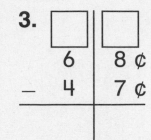

$$
\begin{array}{r}
6\ \ 8¢ \\
-\ 4\ \ 7¢ \\
\hline
\end{array}
$$

4.
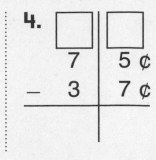

$$
\begin{array}{r}
7\ \ 5¢ \\
-\ 3\ \ 7¢ \\
\hline
\end{array}
$$

5.

$$
\begin{array}{r}
5\ \ 7¢ \\
-\ 1\ \ 9¢ \\
\hline
\end{array}
$$

6.
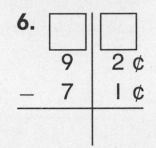

$$
\begin{array}{r}
9\ \ 2¢ \\
-\ 7\ \ 1¢ \\
\hline
\end{array}
$$

7.
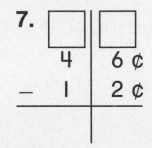

$$
\begin{array}{r}
4\ \ 6¢ \\
-\ 1\ \ 2¢ \\
\hline
\end{array}
$$

8.
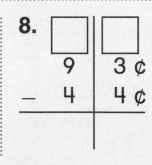

$$
\begin{array}{r}
9\ \ 3¢ \\
-\ 4\ \ 4¢ \\
\hline
\end{array}
$$

9. Jane has 89¢ in her pocket.
She buys a teddy bear pin for 76¢.
How much money does Jane have left?

13¢   14¢   15¢   16¢
Ⓐ   Ⓑ   Ⓒ   Ⓓ

10. Journal Write a story for this problem: 55¢
Then solve the problem.   − 49¢

_____

_____

_____

_____

Estimating Sums

Use mental math to **estimate.**

and

Think: Add the tens first.

20¢ and 10¢ is ⣀30⣀¢.

Think: Add the ones next.

⣀2⣀¢ and ⣀6⣀¢ is ⣀8⣀¢ more.

You have 40¢.

Do you have enough money?

(yes)   no

Estimate. Circle **yes** or **no** to answer the question.

1.

and

_____¢ and _____¢ is _____¢.

_____¢ and _____¢ is _____¢ more.

You have 50¢.

Do you have enough money?

yes   no

2.

and

_____¢ and _____¢ is _____¢.

_____¢ and _____¢ is _____¢ more.

You have 60¢.

Do you have enough money?

yes   no

Estimating Sums and Differences

Estimate. Circle **yes** or **no** to answer the question.

37¢   12¢   49¢   30¢   24¢

1. Can you buy and with 50¢?

    (yes)

    no

2. Can you buy 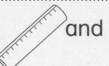 and with 70¢?

    yes

    no

Estimate. Circle **more** or **less** to answer the question.

3. You have 80¢.

You buy .   more

Will you have more   less
or less than 30¢?

4. You have 60¢.

You buy [ruler].   more

Will you have more   less
or less than 40¢?

5. Reanna wants to buy the ruler and the lock.
About how much money does she need?

Ⓐ   about 30¢   Ⓒ   about 50¢

Ⓑ   about 40¢   Ⓓ   about 60¢

6. Reasoning Sam has 45¢. He has exactly enough
money to buy the lock for 30¢ and an apple.
How much does the apple cost?

    10¢   15¢   20¢   25¢
    Ⓐ   Ⓑ   Ⓒ   Ⓓ

Name _____

Problem Solving: Try, Check, and Revise

Use the chart to solve the problem.

Animal Stickers	
Animal	**Price**
Elephant	33¢
Lion	18¢
Tiger	25¢
Zebra	21¢

Ken collects animal stickers.
He paid 43¢ for two stickers.
Which stickers did he buy?

Find two stickers that add up to 43¢.

Try: Pick two numbers.   25¢ and 21¢
             Add the numbers.   25¢ + 21¢ = 46¢

Check: Is the sum 43¢? No.

Revise: Pick two other numbers.   18¢ and 25¢
             Add the numbers.   18¢ + 25¢ = 43¢
             Is the sum 43¢? Yes.

Ken bought the lion and tiger stickers.

Use the chart to solve the problem.
Try, check, and revise (if necessary.)

I. Nina paid 51¢ for two stickers. Which stickers did she buy?

Try: 33¢ and 21¢

Check: 33¢ + 21¢ = 54¢

           Is the sum 51¢? No .

Revise: 33¢ + _____ = _____

Nina bought the _____ and _____ stickers.

Name _____

Problem Solving: Try, Check, and Revise

Use the chart to solve.
Try, check, and revise
(if you need to)
to solve each problem.

Dog Treat Prices	
Dog Treat	**Price**
Biscuit	36¢
Bone	34¢
Twist	29¢
Stick	23¢

1. Suppose Marty paid 2 quarters, 1 dime, and 1 nickel for two dog treats. Which two treats did she buy?

Ⓐ biscuit and bone   Ⓒ bone and stick

Ⓑ twist and biscuit   Ⓓ stick and twist

2. Abdul paid 50¢ and got 27¢ in change. Which dog treat did he buy?

biscuit   bone   twist   stick
Ⓐ   Ⓑ   Ⓒ   Ⓓ

3. Geometry Jill paid 75¢ for a ring.
She got 7¢ in change.
Which type of stone does her ring have?

Ⓐ

Ⓑ ○

Ⓒ △

Ⓓ

Ring Prices	
Stone Shape	**Price**
Square	62¢
Circle	54¢
Triangle	68¢
Rectangle	79¢

Exploring Length

CRAYON

Look at the crayon.
About how many cubes long is the crayon?

When you **estimate** how long something is, you make a good guess.

Estimate.

I think the crayon is about _____ cubes long.

Then measure using cubes.

The crayon is about ___5___ cubes long.

CRAYON

Estimate the length of each object.
Then measure using cubes.

I. I think the car is about _____ cubes long.

The car is about _____ cubes long.

2. I think the ribbon is about _____ cubes long.

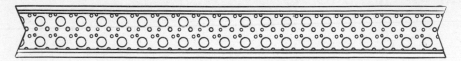

The ribbon is about _____ cubes long.

R 15·1

Name _____

Exploring Length

Estimate the length of each line.
Then use paper clips to measure.

1. ▬▬▬▬▬▬▬▬▬▬▬▬▬▬▬

Estimate: about ___4___ paper clips

Measure: about ___4___ paper clips

2. ▬▬▬▬▬▬▬▬▬

Estimate: about _____ paper clips

Measure: about _____ paper clips

Use paper clips to measure. About how long is each animal's picture?

3.

(A) 1 paper clip long

(B) 2 paper clips long

(C) 3 paper clips long

(D) 4 paper clips long

4.

(A) 4 paper clips long

(B) 3 paper clips long

(C) 2 paper clips long

(D) 1 paper clip long

5. Spatial Thinking Circle the longest worm.

Name _____

Inches

Use a ruler to measure inches.

> To measure to the nearest inch, look at the halfway mark between inches. If the object is longer, use the greater number. If the object is shorter, use the lesser number.

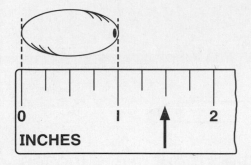

The bead is about

_1_ inch long.

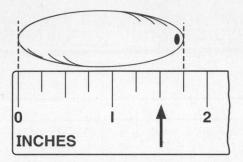

The bead is about

_2_ inches long.

1. Journal Find something in the classroom to measure in inches. Draw the object and write the measurement to the nearest inch.

Estimate the height or length.
Then use a ruler to measure.

2. height of a book

My Favorite Book

Estimate	Measure
about _____ inches	about _____ inches
about _____ inches	about _____ inches

3. length of a pencil

Inches

Estimate the length of each object.
Then use a ruler to measure.

1.

Estimate: about _____ inches

Measure: about _____ inches

2.

Estimate: about _____ inches

Measure: about _____ inches

3.

Estimate: about _____ inches

Measure: about _____ inches

4.

Estimate: about _____ inches

Measure: about _____ inches

5. **Reasonableness.** Measure the length of the straw in inches.
About how long is the straw?

Ⓐ about 5 inches   Ⓒ about 7 inches

Ⓑ about 6 inches   Ⓓ about 8 inches

Name _____

Centimeters

Use a ruler to measure centimeters.

To measure to the nearest centimeter, look at the halfway mark between centimeters. If the object is longer, use the greater number. If the object is shorter, use the smaller number.

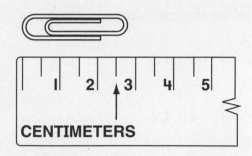

CENTIMETERS

The paper clip is about

_3_ centimeters.

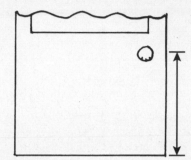

This part of the door is about

_100_ centimeters.

I. Writing in Math Find something in the classroom to measure in centimeters. Draw the object and write the measurement to the nearest centimeter.

Estimate the height or length.
Then use a ruler to measure.

2. length of a
tape dispenser

3. height of
a book

Estimate	Measure
about ____ centimeters	about ____ centimeters
about ____ centimeters	about ____ centimeters

R 15·3

Centimeters

Estimate the length of each object.
Then use a ruler to measure.

1.
Estimate: about _____ cm

Measure: about _____ cm

2. Estimate: about _____ cm

Measure: about _____ cm

3.
Estimate: about _____ cm

Measure: about _____ cm

4. Look at the spoon. Measure the length of the spoon in centimeters. About how long is the spoon?

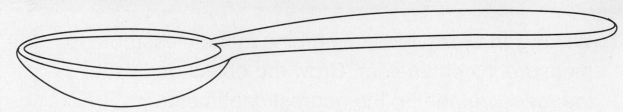

Ⓐ about 10 centimeters   Ⓒ about 16 centimeters

Ⓑ about 13 centimeters   Ⓓ about 18 centimeters

5. **Spatial Thinking** Choose the object that is about 1 centimeter long.

Ⓐ   Ⓒ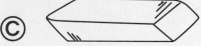

Ⓑ    Ⓓ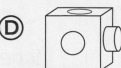

Inches, Feet, and Yards

This rope is about 1 inch long.

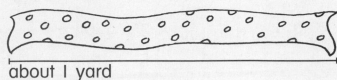

about 1 inch

This ribbon is about 1 foot long.
There are 12 inches in 1 foot.

about 1 foot

This scarf is about 1 yard long.
There are 3 feet in 1 yard.

about 1 yard

About how long is each object? Circle the answer.

1.

about 1 inch

about 1 foot

about 1 yard

2.

about 1 inch

about 1 foot

about 1 yard

3.

about 1 inch

about 1 foot

about 1 yard

4.

about 1 inch

about 1 foot

about 1 yard

---

5. Estimation About how long is the piece of tape?

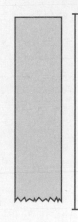

about 1 inch   about 2 inches   about 6 inches

Name _____

Inches, Feet, and Yards

Circle the object that is about each length.

1. a foot

2. a yard

3. an inch

4. Measure from your fingertips to your elbow.

Estimate	Measure	Standard Units
about _____ paper clips	about _____ paper clips	about _____ inches

5. Sandy measures the length of a hockey stick. She says it is 4 units long. What unit did she use?

Ⓐ cubes

Ⓑ inches

Ⓒ feet

Ⓓ yards

6. **Reasonableness** What is the height of the water bottle?

Ⓐ 9 cubes

Ⓑ 9 inches

Ⓒ 9 feet

Ⓓ 9 yards

Name _____

Centimeters and Meters

This bead is about 1 centimeter long.

about 1 centimeter

There are 100 centimeters in 1 meter.
You would need 100 of these beads to make 1 meter!

 ...

About how long is each object?
Circle the answer.

1.
about 1 centimeter

about 1 meter

2.
about 1 centimeter

about 1 meter

3.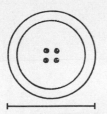
about 1 centimeter

about 1 meter

4.
about 3 centimeters

about 3 meters

R 15·5

Name _____

Centimeters and Meters

Circle the object that is about each length.

1. I centimeter

2. I meter

3. I centimeter

4. Which line is about I centimeter long?

Ⓐ _____

Ⓑ _____

Ⓒ ___

Ⓓ __

5. Algebra How long are these 2 cubes joined together?
Write the missing numbers. Then add.

____ + ____ = ____ centimeters

Measuring Length

You can measure using different units.

Derrick measured the gift box in inches
and in feet.

The gift box is about _____ inches long.

The gift box is about _____ foot long.

It takes more inches than feet to measure the gift box.
If you use smaller units, you need to use more.

Measure each object using different units.
Circle the unit you need more of to measure
each object.

1.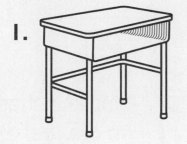

about _____ feet   about _____ yards

more feet

more yards

2.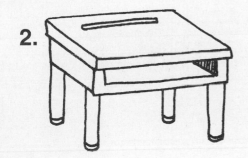

about _____ inches   about _____ feet

more inches

more feet

Measuring Length

You can use different units to measure.

Use different units to measure classroom objects like the ones pictured below. Then circle the unit you need more of to measure each object.

1.

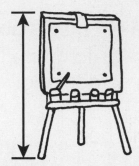

more feet
more yards

about ____ feet

about ____ yards

2.

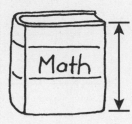

more inches
more feet

about ____ feet

about ____ inches

3.

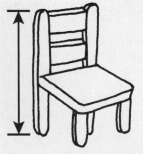

more inches
more feet

about ____ feet

about ____ inches

4.

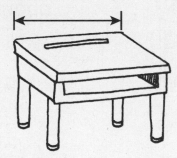

more inches
more feet

about ____ inches

about ____ feet

Adding and Subtracting in Measurement

You can use addition and subtraction to solve problems with measurements.

How much longer is the snake than the worm?

18 in.

6 in.

⟨Think: Subtract to compare.⟩

$18 - 6 = 12$ 12 in. longer

Solve each problem.
Write a number sentence. Then write the solution.

1. What is the distance around the flat surface of the game box?

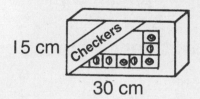

15 cm

Checkers

30 cm

$30 + 15 + \underline{} = \underline{}$

Distance around: _____ cm

2. **Writing in Math** Did you add or subtract in Exercise 1? Explain.

_____

_____

_____

_____

Adding and Subtracting in Measurement

Write a number sentence to solve each problem.

1. What is the distance around the rug?

28 in.

15 in. _____

Distance around: _____ in.

....

2. How much shorter is the feather than the ribbon?

7 cm

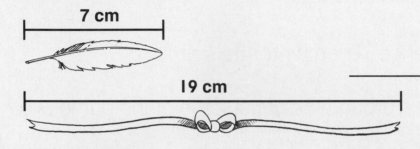

19 cm

_____

_____ cm shorter

....

3. Algebra Which number sentence shows the distance around the cover of the DVD case?

14 cm

Tim's
Camping Trip

19 cm

Ⓐ 14 cm + 19 cm + 14 cm = 47 cm

Ⓑ 14 cm + 19 cm + 14 cm + 19 cm = 66 cm

Ⓒ 19 cm + 14 cm = 33 cm

Ⓓ 19 cm − 14 cm = 5 cm

Comparing Length

What is the total length of the path?

Path A

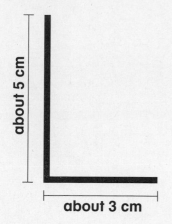

Measure each part of a
path to find the total length.

$\underline{3} + \underline{5} = \underline{8}$

The path is __8__ centimeters long.

Use a centimeter ruler to measure the path.

I. Path B

___ + ___ = ___

____ centimeters long

2. Which path is longer? Circle the answer.

Path A   Path B

3. How much longer is the longer path?

____ centimeter

Comparing Lengths

Use a centimeter ruler to measure each path.

1. Path A

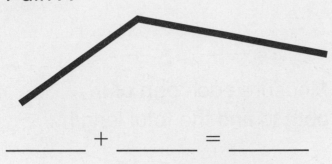

_____ + _____ = _____

_____ centimeters long

2. Path B

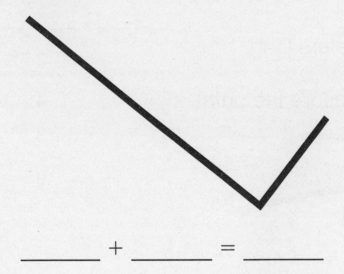

_____ + _____ = _____

_____ centimeters long

3. Which path is longer? Circle the answer.

Path A   Path B

4. Complete.

Path _____ is _____ centimeters longer than Path _____.

Problem Solving: Use Objects

You can use a string to measure a path that is not straight. First, place the string on top of the path. Then, use a ruler to measure the string.

The path is about __6__ inches long.

Use string to measure the path.
Then measure the string with a ruler.

1. The path is about __3__ inches long.

2. The path is about ____ inches long.

Problem Solving: Use Objects

Measure each path.

1.

about _____ inches

2.

about _____ inches

3.

about _____ inches

4.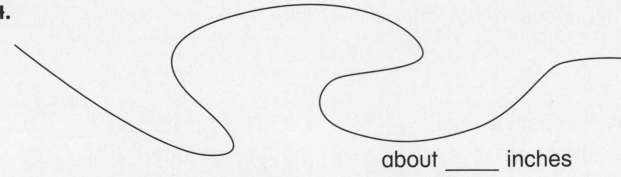

about _____ inches

5. Reasoning Mrs. Green sews these patterns on cloth with thread using her sewing machine. She needs to know how much thread to buy. Which pattern does she need to measure with string?

Ⓐ

Ⓒ

Ⓑ

Ⓓ

Telling Time to Five Minutes

To tell time to five minutes, count by 5s for every number.

The time is

4:25.

There are 30 minutes in a half hour and 60 minutes in an hour.

The time is

4:30.

The hour hand moves from number to number in 60 minutes.

The time is

5:15.

Count by 5s.
Write the time.

1.

2.

3.

4.

R 16·1

Name _____

Telling Time to Five Minutes

Write the time.

1.

2.

3.

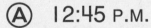
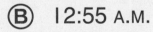

4.

5. The time is 6:05. What number would the
minute hand be pointing to on a clock?

       6   5   2   1

       Ⓐ   Ⓑ   Ⓒ   Ⓓ

6. The clock shows the time I ate lunch.
What time does it show?

Ⓐ 12:45 P.M.   Ⓒ 12:55 P.M.

Ⓑ 12:55 A.M.   Ⓓ 1:00 A.M.

7. Number Sense Look at the time on the first clock.
What time will it be in five minutes?
Show that time on the second clock.

Name _____

Telling Time Before and After the Hour

There are different ways to say time before and after the hour.

6:15	6:30	6:45	2:35
15 minutes after 6 or **quarter past** 6	30 minutes after 6 or **half past** 6	45 minutes after 6 or **quarter to** 7	25 minutes **before** 3 or 35 minutes after 2

Count by 5s to tell the time. Write the time.

1. 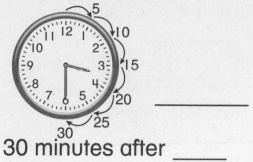 _____

30 minutes after _____

or **half past** _____

2.  _____

15 minutes after _____

or **quarter past** _____

3. Reasoning The time is 6:10. Is the hour hand closer to 6 or 7? Why?

_____

_____

Telling Time Before and After the Hour

Write the time or draw the hands to show the time.
Then write the time before or after the hour.

1.

quarter to ___11___

2.

half past _____

3. Joyce gets up at ten minutes before 7 A.M. Which clock shows this time?

Ⓐ

Ⓑ

Ⓒ

Ⓓ

4. Journal Write two ways to say the time shown.

_____

_____

_____

_____

Name _____

Using a Calendar

This calendar shows the month of March.
The list shows the months of the year in order.

January
February
March
April
May
June
July
August
September
October
November
December

Days of the week

Name of the month

Dates in this month

March						
Sunday	Monday	Tuesday	Wednesday	Thursday	Friday	Saturday
	1	2	3	4	5	6
7	8	9	10	11	12	13
14	15	16	17	18	19	20
21	22	23	24	25	26	27
28	29	30	31			

Look at the last date in the month to find how many days in march.

There are __12__ months.

March is the __3rd__ month of the year.

There are __31__ days in March.

Use the calendar and list to solve the problems.

1. There are 52 weeks in a year. There are __5__ weeks in March.

2. What is the day after Wednesday? _____

3. What day is the 16th of March? _____

4. What is the date of the last Sunday in March? _____

5. What is the last month of the year? _____

Using a Calendar

Use the calendar to solve the problems.

January						
S	M	T	W	T	F	S
						1
2	3	4	5	6	7	8
9	10	11	12	13	14	15
16	17	18	19	20	21	22
23	24	25	26	27	28	29
30	31					

February						
S	M	T	W	T	F	S
		1	2	3	4	5
6	7	8	9	10	11	12
13	14	15	16	17	18	19
20	21	22	23	24	25	26
27	28					

March						
S	M	T	W	T	F	S
		1	2	3	4	5
6	7	8	9	10	11	12
13	14	15	16	17	18	19
20	21	22	23	24	25	26
27	28	29	30	31		

April						
S	M	T	W	T	F	S
					1	2
3	4	5	6	7	8	9
10	11	12	13	14	15	16
17	18	19	20	21	22	23
24	25	26	27	28	29	30

May						
S	M	T	W	T	F	S
1	2	3	4	5	6	7
8	9	10	11	12	13	14
15	16	17	18	19	20	21
22	23	24	25	26	27	28
29	30	31				

June						
S	M	T	W	T	F	S
			1	2	3	4
5	6	7	8	9	10	11
12	13	14	15	16	17	18
19	20	21	22	23	24	25
26	27	28	29	30		

July						
S	M	T	W	T	F	S
					1	2
3	4	5	6	7	8	9
10	11	12	13	14	15	16
17	18	19	20	21	22	23
24	25	26	27	28	29	30
31						

August						
S	M	T	W	T	F	S
	1	2	3	4	5	6
7	8	9	10	11	12	13
14	15	16	17	18	19	20
21	22	23	24	25	26	27
28	29	30	31			

September						
S	M	T	W	T	F	S
				1	2	3
4	5	6	7	8	9	10
11	12	13	14	15	16	17
18	19	20	21	22	23	24
25	26	27	28	29	30	

October						
S	M	T	W	T	F	S
						1
2	3	4	5	6	7	8
9	10	11	12	13	14	15
16	17	18	19	20	21	22
23	24	25	26	27	28	29
30	31					

November						
S	M	T	W	T	F	S
		1	2	3	4	5
6	7	8	9	10	11	12
13	14	15	16	17	18	19
20	21	22	23	24	25	26
27	28	29	30			

December						
S	M	T	W	T	F	S
				1	2	3
4	5	6	7	8	9	10
11	12	13	14	15	16	17
18	19	20	21	22	23	24
25	26	27	28	29	30	31

Spatial Thinking

1. What month comes just before May? __April__

2. What month comes just after August? _____

3. What day of the week is December 3? _____

4. Sara's birthday is in a month that has 5 Thursdays.
Her birthday is on a Thursday, and is the 23rd of the month.
What month is her birthday on this calendar?

Ⓐ June   Ⓒ August

Ⓑ September   Ⓓ December

Name _____

Equivalent Times

"Equivalent" is another way to say "the same" or "equal to."
There are different ways to say the same amount of time.

 minutes is the same as 1 hour.

I day is equal to _24_ hours.

I year is equivalent to _12_ months.

I year is equivalent to _52_ weeks.

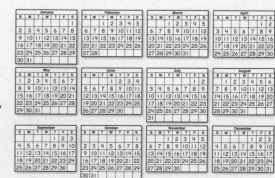

Circle the equivalent times.

1. Mario reads for 1 hour.

　30 minutes　　　　60 minutes　　　　120 minutes

2. Erin was on vacation for 7 days.

　1 week　　　　1 month　　　　1 year

3. Debbie's family lived in California for 1 year.

　1 week　　　　7 weeks　　　　52 weeks

R 16-4

Equivalent Times

Equivalent Times			
I hour	60 minutes	I year	12 months
I day	24 hours	I year	52 weeks
I week	7 days		

1. Jorge went to art class for I hour. How many minutes was art class?

_____

2. Oak School had classes for 36 weeks. Is that more than I year or less than I year?

_____

3. David made muffins from 2 P.M. until 4 P.M. How much time did he spend making muffins? Tell two ways.

_____

4. Lisa played on a soccer team for two years. How many months did she play on the soccer team?

_____

5. **Reasoning** Which two units of time are **NOT** equivalent?

Ⓐ 60 minutes and I hour   Ⓒ I year and 52 weeks

Ⓑ I week and 8 days   Ⓓ 12 months and I year

P 16·4

Organizing Data

Use this data to make a bar graph.

Children at Grand School sold
tickets to their school play.

| Grade 1 sold 8 tickets. |
| Grade 2 sold 15 tickets. |
| Grade 3 sold 12 tickets. |

Color the boxes to show the
number of tickets each grade sold.

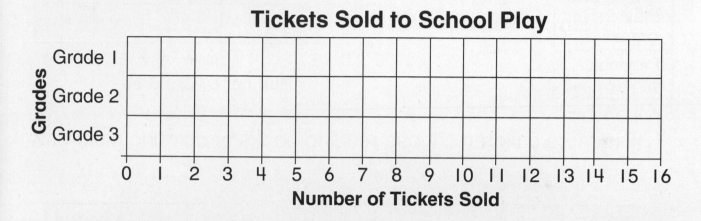

Tickets Sold to School Play

Use the bar graph to compare data.

1. How many tickets did Grade 3 sell? __12__

2. How many tickets did Grade 1 sell? _____

3. Which grade sold the fewest tickets? _____

4. Which grade sold the most tickets? _____

5. How many more tickets did Grade 3 sell than Grade 1? _____

6. Which grade sold more than 13 tickets? _____

Name _____

Organizing Data

Use the table to make the bar graph.
Then use the bar graph to solve the problems.

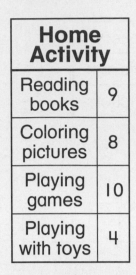

Home Activity	
Reading books	9
Coloring pictures	8
Playing games	10
Playing with toys	4

1. Did more children choose reading books or coloring pictures?

_____

2. Which activity is the favorite of the greatest number of children?

_____

3. Which activity is the favorite of the fewest number of children?

_____

4. **Estimation** About how many children were asked to vote for their favorite home activity?

Ⓐ about 10 children

Ⓒ about 30 children

Ⓑ about 20 children

Ⓓ about 40 children

Graphing Lengths

The table shows the lengths of objects in inches.

Object	Length in Inches
Spoon	5
Knife	8
Fork	6

Use the data from the table to make a line plot.

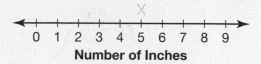

Number of Inches

Use the line plot to answer the questions.

1. Which object is the longest? _____

2. Is the fork longer than the knife or the spoon? _____

3. How can you tell?

_____

_____

4. How much longer is the fork than the spoon?

_____

_____

Name _____

Graphing Lengths

Measure each shoe in inches.

1. Green Shoe

The green shoe is _____ inches long.

....

2. Purple Shoe

The purple shoe is _____ inches long.

....

Complete the table.

Use the data from the table to make a line plot.

Shoe	Length in Inches
Red	4
Green	
Purple	

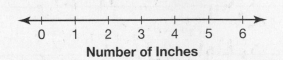

Number of Inches

Use the line plot to answer the question.

3. How many inches shorter is the red shoe than the purple shoe?

    Ⓐ 2   Ⓑ 1   Ⓒ 4   Ⓓ 5

Pictographs

A pictograph uses pictures or symbols to show information. Write how many children chose each snack.

There are 9 symbols for popcorn. So 9 children chose popcorn.

Each ☺ = 1 child

Favorite Snacks

Popcorn	☺☺☺☺☺☺☺☺☺	9
Fruit Cups	☺☺☺☺	___
Yogurt	☺☺☺☺☺☺☺	___
Cheese and Crackers	☺☺☺☺☺☺☺☺☺☺	___

Use the graph to answer the questions.

1. How many children like cheese and crackers best? _____ children

2. How many children like yogurt the best? _____ children

3. Which snack is the least favorite? _____

4. Which snack is favored by most children? _____

5. How many more children like yogurt than fruit cups? _____ children

6. How many more children like cheese and crackers than yogurt? _____ children

Name _____

Pictographs

Use the tally chart to complete the pictograph.
Then use the pictograph to solve the problems.

Shapes	
Circle	✝✝✝
Square	////
Triangle	✝✝✝ ///

Our Favorite Shapes	
1. Circle	
2. Square	
3. Triangle	

4. How many children chose squares? children

5. **Geometry** Which shape is the least favored?

triangle   rectangle   square   circle
Ⓐ   Ⓑ   Ⓒ   Ⓓ

6. Look at the tally chart.
It shows favorite snacks.
Which graph matches
the tally chart?

Our Favorite Snacks	
Banana	/
Crackers	///
Yogurt	//

Ⓐ
Our Favorite Snacks	
Banana	🍌
Crackers	◇◇◇◇
Yogurt	🥤🥤🥤

Ⓒ
Our Favorite Snacks	
Banana	🍌
Crackers	◇◇◇
Yogurt	🥤🥤

Ⓑ
Our Favorite Snacks	
Banana	🍌🍌
Crackers	◇◇◇
Yogurt	🥤🥤

Ⓓ
Our Favorite Snacks	
Banana	🍌🍌
Crackers	◇
Yogurt	🥤🥤🥤

Name _____

Problem Solving: Use a Graph

You can use the data on the graph to solve the problem.

How many more votes did the Tigers get than the Lions?

Votes for Team Name	
Wolves	🐺 🐺 🐺 🐺 🐺
Tigers	🐯 🐯 🐯 🐯 🐯 🐯 🐯 🐯 🐯 🐯 🐯
Lions	🦁 🦁 🦁 🦁 🦁 🦁 🦁 🦁 🦁

Count the Tigers and Lions on the graph.
Then subtract.

$$\underline{11} - \underline{9} = \underline{2}$$

There are __2__ more votes for Tigers than Lions.

Use the graph to solve the problem.
How many more children chose soccer than T-ball?

Game Choices

1. How many children chose soccer? __9__

2. How many children chose T-ball? _____

3. Subtract. _____ – _____ = _____ children

Problem Solving: Use a Graph

Use the bar graph to answer the questions.

Favorite Ice Cream

Kinds of Ice Cream		0	1	2	3	4	5	6	7	8	9	10
	Vanilla											
	Chocolate											
	Strawberry											

Number of Children

1. Which ice cream got the most votes? __chocolate__

2. Which ice cream is least favored? _____

3. How many children voted? _____ children

4. Use the picture graph.
   How many children like blue best?

   Ⓐ 2 children

   Ⓑ 3 children

   Ⓒ 4 children

   Ⓓ 5 children

Favorite Colors

Red	Blue	Green
☺☺☺☺	☺☺☺☺☺	☺☺

5. **Journal** What does the picture graph show?

_____

_____

_____

Writing Multiplication Stories

You can draw a picture and write a story to show 2 × 3.
Draw 2 fish tanks.
Draw 3 fish in each tank.
Solve the story.

There are __2__ tanks.

There are __3__ fish in each tank.

How many fish in all? 2 × 3 = __6__

Finish the picture and the story for 6 × 3.

1.

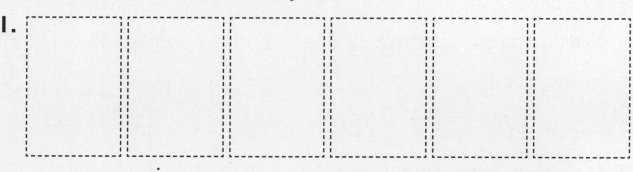

There are __6__ boxes.

There are _____ in each box.

How many _____ in all? 6 × 3 = ____

2. Journal Draw a picture and write a story about 4 × 2.

Name _____

Writing Multiplication Stories

Draw a picture. Write a story and solve.

1. $4 \times 2 =$

2. $5 \times 3 =$ _____

_____

_____

_____

_____

_____

_____

3. Margot has 4 pencil holders. Each one holds 3 pencils. Which number sentence shows how many pencils Margot has?

$3 \times 3 = 9$ $\quad$ $4 \times 4 = 16$ $\quad$ $4 \times 3 = 12$ $\quad$ $3 \times 5 = 15$
Ⓐ $\qquad\qquad$ Ⓑ $\qquad\qquad$ Ⓒ $\qquad\qquad$ Ⓓ

4. Journal Jeb drew this picture to show 3×8. Write a story about the picture. Solve.

_____

_____

_____

$3 \times 8 =$ _____

Name _____

Division as Sharing

5 children want to share 10 counters equally. Draw 1 counter for each child. Keep drawing 1 counter for each child until you have drawn 10 counters in all.

If each child gets the same number of counters, each gets an **equal share.**

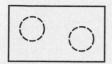 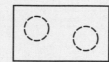 

| Brandon | Melissa | Joaquin | Dorothea | Janet |

There are __10__ counters to share equally.

There are __5__ groups of counters.

There are __2__ counters in each group.

Each child gets __2__ counters.

Draw to show equal groups.
Write how many each child gets.

1. 4 children want to share 12 counters.

         [ ]

| Gabriel | Talia | Shane | Natanya |

Each child gets _____ counters.

Name _____

Division as Sharing

Make equal groups. Write the numbers.

1. 15 crackers shared by 3 friends

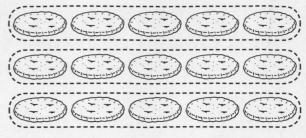

_15_ in all

_3_ groups of _5_ crackers

---

2. 12 books shared by 4 friends

____ in all

____ groups of ____ books

---

3. 21 fish are shared equally by 7 bear cubs.
How many fish does each bear cub get?

    1   2   3   4
    Ⓐ   Ⓑ   Ⓒ   Ⓓ

---

4. Number Sense You have 18 plums. Can you
find 6 different ways to show equal groups?

____ group of ____   ____ groups of ____

____ groups of ____   ____ groups of ____

____ groups of ____   ____ groups of ____

Name _____

Writing Division Stories

Look at the picture.
Read the story.
Then write a division sentence.

There are 15 pilots.
There is an equal number
of pilots in 5 planes.
How many pilots are in each plane?

$$\underset{\text{pilots}}{15} \div \underset{\text{planes}}{5} = \underset{\text{pilots in each plane}}{3}$$

15 divided by 5 is 3.

Look at the picture. Complete the story.
Use the picture to solve the division sentence.

1. A plane has 24 seats in one section.

There are __3__ seats in each row.
How many rows of seats are there?

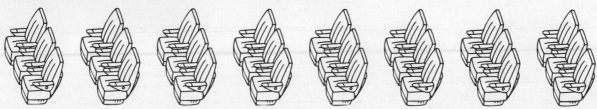

24 ÷ 3 = _____ rows of seats

2. Journal Write a division story for the number sentence
16 ÷ 4 = _____. Solve the division sentence.

Name _____

Writing Division Stories

Draw a picture for the problem.
Then write a division sentence.

1. Alma has 9 shirts. She has
3 drawers. She puts the same
number of shirts in each drawer.
How many shirts does she put
in each drawer?

__9__ ÷ __3__ = __3__

__3__ shirts

2. Felix divides 14 comic books into 2 piles.
Which shows how many comic books are in each pile?

2	4	7	9
Ⓐ	Ⓑ	Ⓒ	Ⓓ

3. Journal Draw a picture. Write a story.
Use the picture to solve the problem.

_____

_____

_____

_____

_____

$18 ÷ 3 =$ _____

Relating Multiplication and Division

Zoe put 12 apples in baskets.
She put 3 apples in each basket.
How many baskets did she use?

12 ÷ 3 = ___?___

Multiplication can help you solve the problem.
Zoe has 12 apples in 4 groups of 3.

So, ___3___ × ___4___ = ___12___

Zoe used ___4___ baskets.   12 ÷ 3 = ___4___

Draw a picture to solve. Write the
multiplication sentence that helps you solve.
Then write the division sentence.

1. Karl puts 10 balls on shelves.
   There are 5 balls on each shelf.
   How many shelves does Karl fill?

   5 × ___2___ = 10

   10 ÷ 5 = ___?___   ___ ÷ ___ = ___

2. Julio has 16 cards.
   He puts 4 cards in each row.
   How many rows are there?

   4 × ___ = ___

   16 ÷ 4 = ___?___   ___ ÷ ___ = ___

Relating Multiplication and Division

Complete each sentence. Use counters if you need to.

1. $2 \times \underline{8} = 16$

   $16 \div 2 = \underline{8}$

2. $4 \times \underline{} = 20$

   $20 \div 4 = \underline{}$

3. $4 \times \underline{} = 12$

   $12 \div 4 = \underline{}$

4. $7 \times \underline{} = 21$

   $21 \div 7 = \underline{}$

5. $5 \times \underline{} = 25$

   $25 \div 5 = \underline{}$

6. $9 \times \underline{} = 18$

   $18 \div 9 = \underline{}$

7. $4 \times \underline{} = 8$

   $8 \div 4 = \underline{}$

8. $5 \times \underline{} = 15$

   $15 \div 5 = \underline{}$

9. Which array shows both $2 \times 3 = 6$ and $6 \div 2 = 3$?

Ⓐ

Ⓑ

Ⓒ

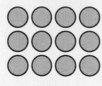
Ⓓ

10. **Algebra** Which multiplication sentence will help you complete $24 \div 8 = \underline{}$?

$4 \times 4 = 16$ $8 \times 3 = 24$ $8 \times 4 = 32$ $8 \times 8 = 64$
    Ⓐ   Ⓑ   Ⓒ   Ⓓ

Unit Fractions and Regions

A fraction can name one of the equal parts of a whole shape.

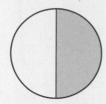 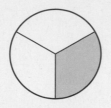 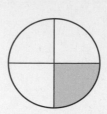

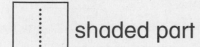 shaded part

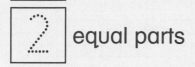 equal parts

$\frac{1}{2}$ is shaded.

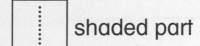 shaded part

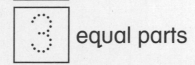 equal parts

$\frac{1}{3}$ is shaded.

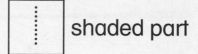 shaded part

equal parts

$\frac{1}{4}$ is shaded.

Color one part. Write how many shaded and equal parts.
Write the fraction.

1.

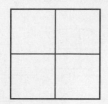

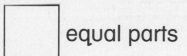 shaded part

equal parts

—— is shaded.

2.

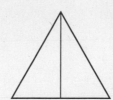

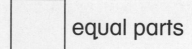 shaded part

equal parts

—— is shaded.

Name _____

Unit Fractions and Regions

Write the fraction for the shaded part of the shape.

1.

$\dfrac{1}{4}$ ___

2.

___

3.

___

4.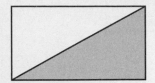

___

5.

___

6.

___

7. Vinnie colored one part of the circle.
What fraction of the circle did he color?

Ⓐ $\dfrac{1}{2}$

Ⓑ $\dfrac{1}{3}$

Ⓒ $\dfrac{1}{4}$

Ⓓ $\dfrac{1}{6}$

8. Algebra Find the fraction for the shaded part of each shape. Look for a pattern. Which shape is missing?

   ___

Ⓐ

Ⓑ

Ⓒ

Ⓓ

Non-Unit Fractions and Regions

A fraction can name two or more equal parts of a whole shape.

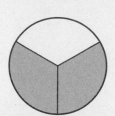 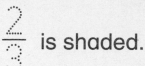

shaded parts

equal parts

$\frac{2}{3}$ is shaded.

Color the parts red.
Write the fraction for the shaded part.

I. Color 4 parts.

☐ red parts

☐ equal parts

is red. ___

2. Color 2 parts.

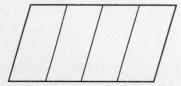

☐ red parts

☐ equal parts

is red. ___

3. Color 5 parts.

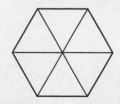

☐ red parts

☐ equal parts

is red. ___

4. Color 3 parts.

☐ red parts

☐ equal parts

is red. ___

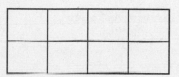

Name _____

Non-Unit Fractions and Regions

Write the fraction for the shaded part of the shape.

1.

$\frac{2}{4}$

2.

_____

3.

_____

4.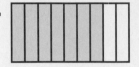

_____

5.

_____

6.

_____

7. Jill has a rug with 8 parts. Four parts are white, and four parts are black. Which shows the rug?

Ⓐ

Ⓑ

Ⓒ

Ⓓ

8. **Geometry** Write the fraction for the shaded part of the rectangle.

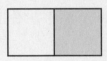

_____

The shaded part is

a _____.

Name _____

Naming Fractions of a Set

A fraction can name the parts of a set.

    $\frac{2}{5}$ shaded balls / balls in all $\frac{2}{5}$ of the balls are shaded.

Color the parts.
Write the fraction for the part you color.

1. Color 2 parts blue.

$\frac{2}{6}$ blue stars / stars in all $\frac{2}{6}$ of the stars are blue.

2. Color 3 parts green.

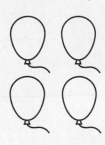 ☐ green balloons / ☐ balloons in all ___ of the balloons are green.

3. Color 5 parts red.

 ☐ red apples / ☐ apples in all ___ of the apples are red.

Name _____

Naming Fractions of a Set

Write the fraction of the set that is shaded.

1.  $\dfrac{4}{5}$

2. 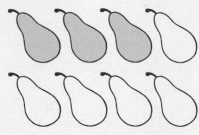 _____

3.  _____

4. 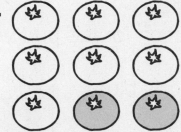 _____

5. What fraction of the bananas are shaded?

Ⓐ $\dfrac{1}{2}$

Ⓑ $\dfrac{4}{7}$

Ⓒ $\dfrac{3}{4}$

Ⓓ $\dfrac{7}{4}$

6. What fraction of the cherries are shaded?

Ⓐ $\dfrac{12}{10}$

Ⓑ $\dfrac{10}{12}$

Ⓒ $\dfrac{2}{12}$

Ⓓ $\dfrac{1}{10}$

7. Number Sense Sue has 9 baseball cards. She gives 4 cards to her brother.

How many cards does Sue have left? _____

What fraction of the cards does Sue have left? _____

Name _____

Showing Fractions of a Set

Show $\frac{2}{3}$ of a set.

How many circles are in the set? __3__

In a fraction, the number in the set is the bottom number. __3__

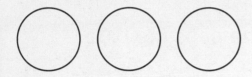

Color 2 circles red.
The top number tells how many circles are red. $\frac{2}{3}$
2 of the 3 circles are red, or $\frac{2}{3}$ of the circles are red.

Color to show the fraction.

1. $\frac{3}{4}$ of the cats are orange.

2. $\frac{1}{5}$ of the dogs are black.

3. $\frac{4}{8}$ of the fish are yellow.

4. $\frac{2}{9}$ of the snakes are green.

5. Journal Draw a set of animals. Then color $\frac{1}{5}$ of the animals.

Name _____

Showing Fractions of a Set

Color to show the fraction.

1. $\frac{3}{4}$ of the houses are red.

2. $\frac{5}{7}$ of the cats are black.

3. $\frac{1}{5}$ of the bows are pink.

4. $\frac{6}{11}$ of the pens are blue.

5. What fraction of the paint jars are shaded?

Ⓐ $\frac{3}{8}$

Ⓑ $\frac{5}{8}$

Ⓒ $\frac{3}{5}$

Ⓓ $\frac{5}{3}$

6. What fraction of the erasers are shaded?

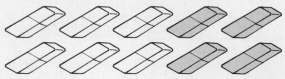

Ⓐ $\frac{4}{10}$

Ⓑ $\frac{6}{10}$

Ⓒ $\frac{4}{6}$

Ⓓ $\frac{2}{10}$

7. Journal Draw and color $\frac{3}{6}$ of a set. Then complete the sentence.

$\frac{3}{6}$ of the _____ are _____.

Name _____

Polygons

Polygons are closed figures that are made up of straight line segments.

Not a polygon
Not a closed
figure

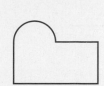
Not a polygon
Not all straight
lines

Polygon
Closed figure
All straight lines

The number of sides in a polygon gives the polygon its name.

Triangle
3 sides

Quadrilateral
4 sides

Pentagon
5 sides

Hexagon
6 sides

Octagon
8 sides

Is each figure a polygon? If it is a polygon, give its name. If not, explain why.

1.
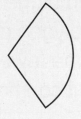

_____

_____

2.

_____

_____

3.
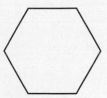

_____

_____

4.

_____

_____

Name _____

Polygons

Name the polygon.

1.   2.    3. 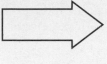   4.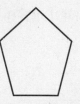

_____   _____   _____   _____

Is each figure a polygon? If it is not, explain why.

5.   6.   7.   8.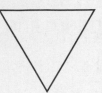

_____   _____   _____   _____

_____   _____   _____   _____

---

9. **Explain It** Juan said that the two figures below are quadrilaterals. Is he correct? Explain.

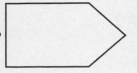

_____

_____

_____

10. **Reasoning** If two of the line segments of a polygon are parallel, what is the fewest number of sides it can have?

_____

---

11. How many more sides does an octagon have than a pentagon?

Ⓐ 1   Ⓑ 2   Ⓒ 3   Ⓓ 4

Adding and Subtracting in Geometry

Debra walks around the sides of her square room.
She takes 12 steps along one side.
How many steps does Debra take?

- Draw the shape.
- Write the length of each side.
- Write a number sentence.
- Use addition or subtraction to solve it.

12 steps

12 steps   12 steps

12 steps

$12 + 12 + 12 + 12 = 48$

Debra takes 48 steps.

Write a number sentence and solve the problem.

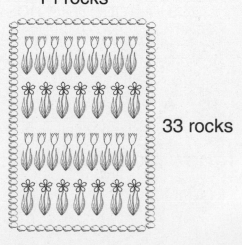

1. The short side of the box is 8 stickers long.
The long side of the box is 17 stickers long.
How many stickers are around this box?

8 stickers   17 stickers

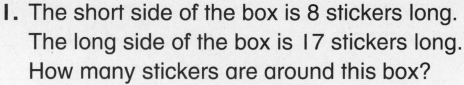

$\underline{8} + \underline{17} + \underline{8} + \underline{17} = \underline{50}$ $\underline{50}$ stickers

---

2. The short side of the garden is
14 rocks long. The long side of the
garden is 33 rocks long. How many
more rocks are on the long side of
the garden than on the short side?

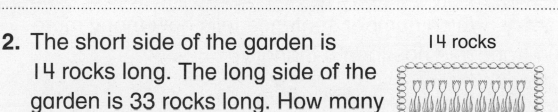

14 rocks

33 rocks

_____ − _____ = _____

_____ more rocks

Name _____

Adding and Subtracting in Geometry

Draw a picture and write a number sentence to solve the problem.

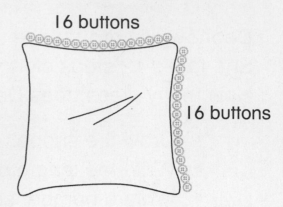

16 buttons

16 buttons

1. Faith makes a square pillow. 16 buttons fit on each side. How many buttons does Faith need in all?

____ + ____ + ____ + ____ = ____   _____ buttons

---

2. Jamie's park is shaped like a rectangle. Jamie takes 63 steps along the short side. He takes 92 steps along the long side. How many more steps is the long side than the short side?

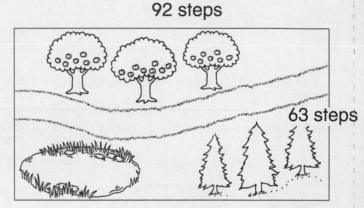

92 steps

63 steps

____ – ____ = ____   _____ more steps

---

3. **Geometry** Which number sentence tells how many more sides a trapezoid has than a triangle?

Ⓐ 5 – 3 = 2   Ⓒ 4 – 3 = 1

Ⓑ 6 – 3 = 3   Ⓓ 6 – 4 = 2